# *WISE UP*
# and
# *EXCEL*

Toyin Jama

# WISE UP and EXCEL

*Nuggets of Wisdom for Winning in the Workplace*

*Nukan Publishing*

# Wise Up and Excel

*(Nuggets of Wisdom for Winning in the Workplace)*



**ISBN 13**: 978-1-906825-04-1

Published by **Nukan Publishing**
**Essex UK**
Email: **admin@nukan.com**

First Printed in **United Kingdom** 2017

**Cover Design**: Design2Impact.co.uk

All Scriptures used in this book are New King James Version unless otherwise indicated. Occasionally, bold-type has been used for emphasis.

# DEDICATION

This book is dedicated to my Lord and Master Jesus Christ

The Author and Finisher of my faith.

My Rock

My Defence

My Shelter

My Protector

My Counsellor

My Friend

My Light

My Shepherd

My Provider

My Peace

My Comfort

My Joy

# ACKNOWLEDGEMENT

I am forever grateful to God and to my family for their amazing support in prayers and encouragement for all my book projects.

To my husband and children – Pastor Joshua Jama for supporting and encouraging me to fulfil God's purpose for my life. Children - Taffat Jama, Emmanuel & Palangfat Adeshipe and Ayo & Fatmohn James – always cheering me on. Thank you all for all the times spent reading my various manuscripts and designs offering valuable comments.

To my mum – Mrs Elizabeth Peters and sisters for your continuous support in prayers and distribution of the books. Thanks Lola for always taking time out to read the first rough manuscripts.

To the wonderful members of Good News Assembly - Manchester, Women of Purpose and Influence Prayer Partners - for continuous encouragement and prayers.

To Pastor Niyi Adeoshun (Nukan Publishing) for taking the raw manuscript and turning it into what you see today at short notice. Thanks for your continuous valuable support regarding the book projects.

# Table of Contents

# INTRODUCTION

*"There are four things which are little on the earth, But they are exceedingly wise: The ants are a people not strong, Yet they prepare their food in the summer; The rock badgers are a feeble folk, Yet they make their homes in the crags; The locusts have no king, Yet they all advance in ranks; The spider skillfully grasps with its hands, And it is in kings' palaces."*

***- Proverbs 30: 24-28***

The bible describes four creatures as exceedingly wise, though little in size compared to other creatures yet considered wise because of what they achieve against all odds. The ants are tiny and delicate yet wise enough to know that they must gather food for themselves in summer against the winter season; basically preparing for when they can't work. The rock badgers work to provide nice accommodation in safe and secure places. The locusts, in their work, make progress with no one supervising them while the spider carefully and skilfully makes its way into king's palaces. Through wisdom all these four creatures are able to achieve the best or reach the top.

Most people spend an average 12 hours a day at work or work-related activities including travelling and preparatory time, which is 75% of our waking hours - assuming 8 hours of sleep. If work takes such a significant percentage of our lives, it is imperative to excel, to be fruitful and be profitable in it; in accordance to God's mandate in Genesis 1:28. "*Then God blessed them, **"Be fruitful and multiply; fill the earth and subdue it;** have dominion over the fish of the sea, over the birds of the air, and over every living thing that moves on the earth"*

Work means anything you are involved in for the betterment of society. It may not necessarily be work for which you get a pay cheque at the end of the month. It includes voluntary work, staying home to raise a family and studying or training for a career. God created mankind in His own image and likeness and put them in charge of every other living things. He commanded them to be fruitful, multiply, replenish and subdue the earth. He gave them total control. The four words – fruitful, multiply, replenish and subdue are all verbs - which are active or *doing* words. It is not a matter of you sleep one day and wake up to find things just happen.

> *"Then God said, "Let Us make man in Our image, according to our likeness; let them have dominion over the fish of the sea, over the birds of the air, and over the cattle, over all the earth and over every creeping thing that creeps on the earth. So God created man in His own image; in the image of God he created him; male and female He created them.* Then God blessed them, "**Be fruitful and multiply; fill the earth and subdue it**; have dominion over the fish of the sea, over the birds of the air, and over every living thing that moves on the earth." - Genesis 1:26-28

God empowered mankind with every ability necessary to accomplish the assignment He has given them. There are specific roles for us to accomplish to fulfil that mandate, there are gardens (Genesis 2:15) He has wired us to cultivate, our job is to seek His face to find out our place in the jigsaw puzzle, to discover where we fit in fulfilling that mandate of Genesis 1:28 to the glory of God and expansion of His kingdom here on earth. See my book "**7 Keys To Accomplishing Your Purpose**" for how to discover and accomplish your purpose.

> *Genesis 2:15 says "Then the Lord God took the man and put him in the Garden of Eden to tend and keep it"*

We need God's wisdom to be able to excel and reign in our work just like the four little creatures who could achieve much through wisdom.

Wisdom is the ability to make a right decision and take the right course of action at a given moment. We've often heard of people described as wise and some as foolish; what distinguish a wise man from a foolish man are their actions. Your actions will tell people if you are wise. Wisdom is practical; it is a way of life.

This book contains wisdom nuggets that will help you excel at work and fulfil your destiny. You will not labour in vain in Jesus' Name. Wisdom nuggets, based on the word of God, will propel us to be the head and not the tail. It is God's will for us to succeed and the word of God contains so many nuggets to help us as indicated in Joshua 1:8 and Deuteronomy 28:13

> *"This Book of the Law shall not depart from your mouth, but you shall meditate in it day and night, that you may observe to do according to all that is written in it. For then you will make your way prosperous, and then you will have good success." - Joshua 1:8*

> *"And the LORD will make you the head and not the tail; you shall be above only, and not be beneath, if you heed the commandments of the LORD your God, which I command you today, and are careful to observe them." - Deuteronomy 28:13*

It doesn't matter your level of attainment in life, you can go higher and achieve more for God, even if you have failed several times and feel your working career has been nothing but a nightmare, I pray the Lord will turn your situation around and you will begin to have victory at your work place in Jesus's name.

> *"The righteous man may fall seven times and rise again." - Proverbs 24:16a.*

A loser remains on the floor and never gets up again but a winner keeps getting up until he can remain standing. We are winners in Christ Jesus, we do not have to remain on the floor. We are on a journey, we have not arrived yet like Paul said in Phil 3:12-14

> *"Not that I have already attained, or am already perfected; but I press on, that I may lay hold of that for which Christ Jesus has already laid hold of me. 13 Brethren, I do not count myself to have apprehended; but one thing I do, forgetting those things which are behind and reaching forward to those things which are ahead, 14 I press toward the goal for the prize of the upward call of God in Christ Jesus." - Philippians 3:12-14.*

We need to keep pressing forward and aspire to succeed. The DNA to succeed is inside of us, 3 John 2 says "*Beloved, I pray that you may prosper in all things and be in health, just as your soul prospers*"

This book is written to make your journey at work smoother. May it impact you to start walking the path of the wise and start making good and godly decisions at work that will glorify God and shape your generations for life.

# CHAPTER 1

# SAY 'YES' TO WISDOM

*"**Get wisdom**! Get understanding! Do not forget, nor turn away from the words of my mouth. Do not forsake her and she will preserve you; Love her, and she will keep you. Wisdom is the principal thing: Therefore **get wisdom**, and in all your getting, get understanding. Exalt her and she will promote you, she will bring you honour when you embrace her. She will place on your head an ornament of grace, a crown of glory she will deliver to you."*
*- Proverbs 4:5-9*

The above scripture admonishes us that when wisdom is appreciated and revered, it will cause us to excel, be promoted and reach the heights God intended for us. The very things we desire when we go to work, are available when we apply the wisdom of God. We not only want to gain employment or establish businesses but to excel and reach the top as God intends for us.

It is through wisdom that God was able to establish the world – heaven and earth and all that is within it (*Proverbs 3:19-20*). Everything was intricately put together by wisdom, no misfit, no disjoint, everything in order, day and night in synchronism. It is through wisdom king Solomon said a house can be built, established, furnished and occupied (*Proverbs 24:3-4*).

> For it *is "through wisdom God founded the earth and by understanding establish the heavens and by*

*knowledge the depths were broken up and clouds drop down the dew." - Proverbs 3:19-20*

*"Through wisdom a house is built, and by understanding it is established; by knowledge the rooms are filled with all precious and pleasant riches." - Proverbs 24:3-4*

The bible describes a happy/blessed man as someone who finds wisdom and gain understanding. We can acquire a million dollars in a brief time but if we don't have wisdom regarding what to do with the money, it will disappear overnight. People have failed in marriages, businesses and ministries for lack of wisdom. So, it is paramount that we pursue wisdom.

*"Happy is the man who **finds wisdom**, And the man who gains understanding; for her proceeds are better than the profits of silver, and her gain than fine gold. She is more precious than rubies, and all the things you may desire cannot compare with her. Length of days is in her right hand, in her left hand riches and honour. Her ways are ways of pleasantness, and all her paths are peace. She is a tree of life to those who take hold of her, and happy are all who retain her."* - Proverbs 3:13-18

If the proceeds of wisdom are better than profits of silver, fine gold, rubies or any other thing that you may desire, we will do ourselves great justice in finding it.

Before you can find something, you need to know what you are looking for. Can you imagine telling people you are looking for something, and they ask you "what are you looking for" and you reply them saying "I don't know", they'll conclude something is wrong with you. So, it is important to understand what wisdom is before searching for it.

## So What Is Wisdom?

To put it simply, wisdom is the ability to make the right decision or choice and act appropriately in a given situation. Wisdom is a lifestyle and it has everything to do with our character. James 3:13 puts it nicely saying *"Who is wise and understanding among you? Let him show by good conduct that his works are done in the meekness of wisdom"*

It is often said actions speak louder than words; you are judged as being wise or foolish by the way you behave. 1 Samuel 18:14-15 says *"And David behaved wisely in all his ways, and the LORD was with him. Therefore, when Saul saw that he behaved very wisely, he was afraid of him"*. King Saul and the people acknowledged the wisdom of David by his actions. You don't need to announce 'I am wise' for people to know you are wise, it is by your actions they will determine if you are wise or not. We can see that king Saul was even afraid of David because of how wise David was, wisdom puts you on another level against your enemy because they do not know how to handle you, for you are always outwitting them irrespective of their schemes and devices.

## Godly Wisdom and Worldly Wisdom.

> *"Who is wise and understanding among you? Let him show by good conduct that his works are done in the meekness of wisdom But if you have bitter envy among and self-seeking in your hearts, do not boast and lie against the truth. This wisdom does not descend from above, but it is earthly, sensual, demonic. For where envy and self-seeking exist, confusion and every evil thing are there. "But the wisdom that is from above is first pure, then*

> *peaceable, gentle, and easy to be entreated, full of mercy and good fruits, without partiality, and without hypocrisy. And the fruit of righteousness is sown in peace of them that make peace" - James 3:13-17.*

Worldly wisdom is about what can **I** get out of people, how **I** can ride on them to get to where **I** want to, it is all about being canny and tricky, smart as the world thinks, it is basically all about **me, myself and I**. The bible clearly describes this as demonic; it leads to confusion and all manner of ills.

However, Godly wisdom is all about glorifying God in our day-to-day living, have you noticed how what characterizes godly wisdom is embodied in the fruit of the Spirit.

> *"But the fruit of the Spirit is love, joy, peace, long-suffering, gentleness, goodness, faith, meekness, temperance: against such there is no law" - Galatians 5:22-23*

Often as Christians we concentrate so much on spiritual gifts and the miraculous and less on the fruit of the spirit. We need the two, they both go hand-in-hand to bring the lost to the Lord. When the world sees us demonstrating the love of God in our characters and in the demonstration of the power of God we will start catching their attention.

Jesus Christ, when He was here on earth, was teaching, preaching, healing, feeding the poor, mixing with the sinners, showing compassion and love; it was a total ministry. It is not about power, power, power and no fruit. Paul said in 2 Corinthians 3:2 *"You are our epistle written in our hearts, known and read by all men".* We are the gospels people are reading daily.

God loves wise people I am not talking of those wise in their own eyes but those who have godly wisdom whereby the fruit of wisdom is manifesting in their lives, i.e. fruit of the spirit and being Christ-like.

> *"For whoever finds me (wisdom) finds life and obtains favour from the Lord." - Proverbs 8:35*

> *"The king's favour is toward a wise servant, but his wrath is against him who causes shame." - Proverb 14:35"*

## How Can We Receive Wisdom?

**Fear God and have reverence for Him:**
God's wisdom is available to those who fear Him and live uprightly. *Proverb 2:6-7 says "For the Lord gives wisdom and from His mouth comes knowledge and understanding. He stores up sound wisdom for the upright; He is a shield to those who walk uprightly".* Walking in the ways of the godly, not in the counsel of the ungodly, following the Lord and obeying His commandments set you up to receive wisdom from God.

Fearing and reverencing God is to realise that He is an awesome, powerful and Holy God. He is supreme, the King of all kings and Lord of all lords. He is Commander-in-Chief and His word is absolute. As we become intimate with God having the right picture of Who He is, wisdom is released. Psalm 111:10 (AMP) says *"The [reverent] fear of the LORD is the beginning (the prerequisite, the absolute essential, the alphabet) of wisdom; A good understanding and a teachable heart are possessed by all those who do the will of the LORD; His praise endures forever."*

> *"The fear of God is the beginning of wisdom and the knowledge of the Holy One is understanding." - Proverbs 9:9.*

.

**Ask God**

> *James 1:5-8 says "If any of you lacks wisdom, let him ask of God who gives to all liberally and without reproach, and it will be given him. But let him ask in faith, with no doubts is like a wave of sea driven and tossed by the wind. For let not that man suppose that he will receive anything from the Lord, he is a double-minded man, unstable in all his ways."*

Asking Him for wisdom acknowledges that we do not have wisdom and we need His wisdom. It confirms our trust in His ability that He knows better and His ways and thoughts for a given situation are better than ours.

> *"For My thoughts are not your thoughts, nor are your ways My ways," says the LORD. "For as the heavens are higher than the earth, so are My ways higher than your ways, And My thoughts than your thoughts" - Isaiah 55:8-9*

This book is about applying Godly wisdom at work so that we can be successful and excel at work – an area where we spend majority of our waking hours.

## CHAPTER 2

# TRUST IN GOD, NOT YOUR BOSS

*"Trust in the LORD with all your heart, and lean not on your own understanding; in all your ways acknowledge Him, And He shall direct your paths."*
*- Proverb 3:5-6*

A wise man is someone who will trust God with all his heart, rather than trusting his own way of seeing an issue, or how wonderful that business proposal looks and how the figures match. A wise man relies on the Lord Who sees from the beginning to the end to reveal if there are any loop-holes in the deal. If we want to be successful in this life, we must follow and trust Him implicitly because part of being wise is trusting in God. A foolish man comes to God with his mind made up, but a wise man lays down his agenda and hears from the all-knowing God.

*"In the fear of the LORD there is strong confidence, and His children will have a place of refuge." - Proverb 14:26*

*"The name of the LORD is a strong tower; the righteous run to it and are safe." - Proverb 18:11*

With so many uncertainties and job insecurities currently in the work place, it is paramount that our trust is in God and not man; that is the only sure way of not being afraid. I work in an industry that is volatile; job security is low and sometimes notice period is one week. You can come in on Monday and be told to finish on Friday. If your faith is not in God, with strong confidence in Him (Proverbs 14:26), it is easy to compromise and do ridiculous things to try and keep a job.

Have you been in an office where people are backbiting, stabbing each other in the back just to be the manager's favourite yet at the end of the day they are still fired? We can't afford to do things the world's way, our refuge should be in the Lord; not our bosses. *Psalm 24:1 says "The earth is the LORD's, and all its fullness, the world and those who dwell therein"* – including your bosses. That needs to be rubber stamped in our spirit man so that we don't operate in fear at work.

> *"My son, let them not depart from your eyes-Keep sound wisdom and discretion; so they will be life to your soul and grace to your neck. Then you will walk safely in your way, and your foot will not stumble. When you lie down, you will not be afraid; yes, you will lie down and your sleep will be sweet. Do not be afraid of sudden terror, nor of trouble from the wicked when it comes; 26 For the LORD will be your confidence, and will keep your foot from being caught."* - Proverbs 3:21-26

If the Lord be for you who can be against you. When you walk in wisdom, living as God commands, you have nothing to fear. You sleep at night like a baby (Proverbs 3:24 talks of sweet sleep) because you know God is in control of your life so you have nothing to fear.

I remember a time I was teaching in a high school where it was customary for the top classes be given to the senior teachers in the department and the not-so-good classes to others. During this time, I was one of two new teachers, so it is clear which classes we would get the following year. Instead of lobbying, I just kept my cool because I knew God would take care of the classes assigned to me. Towards the time of selection, my father died so I had to finish marking my papers in the quickest possible time so I could attend his funeral in Nigeria. I left the class selection to God (Proverbs 16:1-3) knowing that He would work on my behalf. When I came back I was surprised that part of my classes included the top set. God worked on my behalf even when I wasn't even there. It is good to trust the Lord. I have found Him to be faithful at every junction of my life; turning the hearts of kings to my favour (Proverbs 21:1) and bosses being at peace with me (Proverbs 16:7).

I have worked in big corporations where if it is by qualification, I wouldn't be there but because God is in control of my life, He has opened the supernatural doors.

> *"The preparations of the heart belong to man, but the answer of the tongue is from the LORD. All the ways of a man are pure in his own eyes, But the LORD weighs the spirits. Commit your works to the LORD, and your thoughts will be established." - Proverbs 16:1-3*

> *"When a man's ways please the LORD, He makes even his enemies to be at peace with him." - Proverb 16:7*

> *"The king's heart is in the hand of the LORD, like the rivers of water; He turns it wherever He wishes." - Proverb 21:1*

Another verse that keeps me going when the road is rough is

> *"I would have lost heart, unless I had believed that I would see the goodness of the Lord in the land of the living. Wait on the Lord; be of good courage and He shall strengthen your heart" - Psalms 27:13-14*

As a contractor in an industry where contract extensions are dependent upon budgets, there have been times when no one was sure if renewal was going to come through or not. I was at a job for one year and then rumours had it that they were going to *offshore* our duties. There was tension in the atmosphere but the Lord helped me to be at peace. I resolved in my heart that I will be at that job until God says "no more" (Psalm 27:13-14). Eventually after about 2 months, I was told that I was one of the few to be kept in the team. The Lord did it again, God was faithful and my contract was extended by another 6 months.

Towards the end, I was told it looked like there was no more work. I resolved again that I would be here until God says so. My boss even called me to say it looked like that was it to which I replied "no problem"; yet in my heart I resolved **"you are my boss on earth but my heavenly boss will have the last say"**. He called back within 2 weeks to say, they have found room in the budget to keep me on for another 6 months. I am saying all this to affirm that it had only been God and God alone that strengthened my heart not to panic, to be courageous and believe that God will come through for me no matter what, whether at this job or another place.

Proverbs 30:26 says the rock badgers were wise enough to make their homes in the rocky cliffs for security and protection away from dangerous predators. This is how we need to run and hide ourselves in God. The Name of the Lord is a strong tower, the righteous run and they are safe (Proverbs 18:11). At work we need to hide in God for safety during downtimes, when cuts are being implemented everywhere, against economic policies.

When our trust is in God, the solid rock, even when the rain and the snow comes, we will be able to weather the storm. There will be situations that will be challenging at work, where consequence of a missed deadline is dire, but we need to put our faith in the Solid Rock to see us through. There have been times, the rest-room has been my quick exit. I would literally kneel down there to cry out to God for one thing or the other. Other times, I have sat in a meeting and made SOS prayers to the Lord, asking Him to bring peace into a meeting that is going haywire or on occasions when I have been put on the spot to answer a query.

> ***"He alone is my rock and my salvation; he is my fortress, I will not be shaken.*** *My salvation and my honour depend on God; he is my mighty rock, my refuge." - Psalms 62:6-7*

> *"From the ends of the earth I call to you, I call as my heart grows faint; lead me to the rock that is higher than I." - Psalms 61:2*

In a world where there are aggressive deadlines to meet, if you don't have God to go to when you are under extreme pressure, where do you turn to just to take the pressure off temporarily? Substance abuse? Alcohol or affairs? Unfortunately, the consequences after the temporary fix can create further problems.

Putting God first and relying totally on God can help one overcome challenging situation like when people lie and incriminate other people to cover their own mistakes. In law, it is said you are *innocent until proven guilty* but mostly at work you are guilty until proven innocent! I remember a situation where one of the IT security personnel came down to my team to accuse us that a recent activity from our team had caused them to have computer database space issue. Nothing we told this lady would make her budge.

I contacted one of my friends who had experience within similar environment to check if truly our activity could have caused the problem and he said "no". This woman was adamant it was my team. It took another person from her department to do further checks to convince her it wasn't us and proved it was something else. The news had already gone to some quarters and I have a feeling she never communicated the resolution to the people she had spoken to about our team. With situations like this, if my confidence was not in God, I would have felt totally victimized but I knew in my heart it wasn't my team and eventually we were vindicated.

To be able to excel is really to acknowledge God in everything you do at work. Don't leave God out or else the consequence will be dire. It seems we live more and more in challenging workplaces where people will do anything to get to the top. We need to remember that *the weapons of our warfare are not carnal but mighty through God to the pulling of strongholds* (2 Corinthians 10:4) and that if God opened that door for us He will also keep us, we need not be anxious or worried but continue to seek first His kingdom. Matthew 6:31-33 says "*Therefore do not worry, saying, 'What shall we eat?' or 'What shall we drink?' or 'What shall we wear? For after all these things the Gentiles seek. For your heavenly Father knows that you need all these things. But seek first the kingdom of God and His righteousness, and all these things shall be added to you*". God knows our needs and will provide for us at the point of our needs.

In putting God first at work, we need to remember that we have been described in Matthew 5:13-16 as the salt and light in this world and we need to let our light shine so that they may see our good works and glorify the Father. We are the missionaries in the workplace to people who have never been to church in their lives therefore we need to acknowledge Him in the way we do our business and the way we relate with the people so that we do not bring the name of the Lord to disrepute. We are God's ambassadors in the workplace and need to represent Him well. These are principles of being wise and showing in our conduct that we fear God (Proverbs 9:9) and are answerable to Him.

# CHAPTER 3

# COMMUNICATION AT WORK

Effective communication is key to you excelling at work and having a successful career. It is one of the most important business skills we need to acquire and improve upon. Commonly, it is one of the things people look out for on your CV; we often add we have excellent verbal and written communication skills but people tend to also check out for non-verbal communication skills. How we carry ourselves, the eye contact and body language tend to speak volumes than what we put down on paper.

There are different ways of communicating at work, face to face (one on one or in a group), conference calls, emails, texts, WhatsApp, Facebook and company website. Whichever is the means of communication, they carry the same weight in the court of law and can be interpreted by different people at different times so it is important to gain wisdom and understanding into improving our communication skills so that we can excel in what God has committed into our hands.

The principles below apply to whatever means of communication we use; so let's see the mouth to be the same as text/email or whatever we use to communicate our message to the other party.

> *"The heart of the wise teaches his mouth, and adds learning to his lips. Pleasant words are like a*

*honeycomb, Sweetness to the soul and health to the bones." - Proverb 16:23-24*

*"Keep your heart with all diligence for out of it spring the issues of life." - Proverb 4: 23*

*"....Out of the abundance of the heart, the mouth speaks. A good man out of the good treasure of his heart brings forth good things, and an evil man out of the evil treasure brings forth evil things." - Matthew 12:34-35*

The above verses show clearly that the heart and the mouth are uniquely connected and the result of this connection is amazing. The heart is the central processing unit of our lives. It processes what it sees, feels, hears and releases information or feedback to the world through the mouth. If the treasure/content in the heart is good, the mouth will speak forth good things; if it is bad the mouth will speak out bad things. Garbage in garbage out. We are admonished to keep our hearts with all diligence, steadfastly, because out of it flows issues of life, a man is therefore judged as wise or foolish by what proceeds out of his mouth in the following ways.

- The manner or *intonation* of your speech – how you say it.
- The timing of your speech – when you say it.
- The quantity of your speech – how much you say.
- The quality of your speech – the value in what you say.

## The Manner of Your Speech

We can say the right thing in a tone that is harsh, brash, demeaning, or piercing, such that instead of our listener hearing what we are saying, what they hear or receive is negative.

A wise man's words will promote health and progress; will be soft and not harsh; sweet and pleasant to the soul; Gentle and forbearing.

> *"There is one who speaks like the piercing of a sword, but the tongue of the wise promotes health."* - *Proverbs 12:17*

> *"A wise man fears and departs from evil, but a fool rages and is self-confident. Soft answer turns away wrath, but a harsh word stirs up anger. The tongue of the wise uses knowledge rightly, but the mouth of fools pours forth foolishness."* - *Proverb 15:1-2*

> *"By long forbearance a ruler is persuaded, and a gentle tongue breaks a bone."* - *Proverb 25:15*

> *"It is honourable for a man to stop striving, since any fool can start a quarrel."* - *Proverb 20:3*

> *"The heart of the righteous studies how to answer, but the mouth of the wicked pours forth evil." Proverb 15:28*

How piercing do you get with your words? Some people tend revel in being blunt, and they *say it as it is*, but is it really scriptural to wound another person with your tongue? Obviously if you are sensitive to other people's feelings in your heart, if your heart is right towards that person, there is a way you will correct him or her that will not leave the other human being totally in disarray. Proverbs 15:28 says "*the heart of the righteous studies how to answer, it just doesn't pours forth evil.*" He takes care how he ought to answer.

Many relationships would be saved if we think first before we speak. If you have a disposition to be direct in your speech, you may need to be careful how you do this at work because though people may appreciate the direct manner, you will really need to judge your audience. Direct manner of speaking may work for some people but not others. Sometime people can use it to your detriment and set traps or *wind you up* knowing you will be direct. That information may now be used against you later. You can still be direct but be wise about it. Speak the truth in love; the recipient may not be happy but if your motive and manner is right, you will be vindicated eventually. Proverbs 28:23 "*He who rebukes a man will find more favour afterward, than he who flatters with the tongue.*"

## The Timing of Your Speech

Being wise is saying the right thing at the right time. Ecclesiastes 3:7b says *"A time to keep silence and a time to speak".* If we misjudge the timing, the good we are trying to achieve will not be accomplished. Many wrong things have been said *in the heat of the moment* which takes a long time to heal and mend. Many times we would have saved ourselves a lot of trouble if we had only chosen our timing carefully, taken the time not be quick and hasty or exercised self-control. The longer the time we take to cool off, the better we will be able to construct whatever we need to say.

> *"A man has joy by the answer of his mouth, and a word spoken in due season, how good it is!" Proverbs 15:23*

> *"A word fitly spoken is like apples of gold in settings of silver." Proverbs 25:11*

> *"He who is slow to wrath has great understanding, but he who is impulsive exalts folly." - Proverbs14:29*

*"Do you see a man hasty in his words? There is more hope for a fool than for him." - Proverbs 29:20*

*"He who is slow to anger is better than the mighty, and he who rules his spirit than he who takes a city." Proverbs 16:32*

*"The discretion of a man makes him slow to anger, and his glory is to overlook a transgression." Proverbs 19:11*

*"He who answers a matter before he hears it, It is folly and shame to him." - Proverbs 18:13*

We are admonished in 2 Peter 1:5-8 to add to our faith self-control among other fruit of the spirit, for if these things abound in us, we will not be barren nor unfruitful in the knowledge of our Lord Jesus Christ. I am sure you will agree with me that if you look back in your life, many opportunities have been missed because of over-reaction and lack of self-control. I remember the story a man of God told us; he had heard so much about another man of God and he had been wanting to invite him to his church, but they had not had opportunity to meet. Finally at the airport, on his way to a meeting, he saw the famous minister; but as he was going to approach him, he realized the minister was arguing sharply with the reservation clerk. The scene was embarrassing and he just slowly retreated. The fruit of the spirit was not manifesting in the life of this famous minister even though he was mightily anointed. Needless to say, the invitation to minister was not extended to him.

Sometimes it's better to wait a while before answering a situation or email and have time to reflect. It is better to tell the person "I will come back to you, please give me time" or if you have a boss, say you may need to check with them first.

I remember a situation where a Senior Manager called me and was asking why there was a delay on a project, to be honest I wasn't impressed the manager asking me as it wasn't my department's fault why we were delayed. Secondly, I felt he should be speaking to my boss and not me. Apparently, he needed to make a decision about something but I felt in my heart it wasn't my place to give him the answers as I wasn't sure what was going on in the background. I gently told him the status of the work and that my Team Lead would give him more details of what is surrounding the delays as he is aware of more stuff going on in the background. Shortly another person from his team also called and I repeated the same thing. I tried to call my boss to alert him but he was nowhere to be found hence why everyone was frustrated but I felt I should just lay low.

After my initial annoyance, I prayed that the Lord will take control of whatever is going on. Eventually after about 2 hours, I was able to reach my boss, not knowing he was in-flight and obviously couldn't take call, it was then he told me all that had been going on and the guys had no right to have contacted me as it was not my issue even though they were aware he was en-route. This Senior Manager in question had apparently written to our head boss something not exactly true about our team so they are dealing with it. I thank God for the wisdom of God to be calm and not be embroiled in what was going on. If I had allowed pride of feeling important as "the number 2 in command", which I wasn't anyway and try to solve the problem I didn't even know about, I could have gotten all of us into trouble in one way or the other because of impatience.

## The Quantity of Your Speech

> *"In the multitude of words sin is not lacking, but he who restrains his lips is wise" - Proverbs 10:19*

*"He who guards his mouth preserves his life, But he who opens wide his lips shall have destruction." - Proverbs 13:3*

*"He who has knowledge spares his words, and a man of understanding is of a calm spirit. Even a fool is counted wise when he holds his peace; when he shuts his lips, he is considered perceptive." - Proverbs 17:27-28*

*"A fool vents all his feelings but a wise man holds them back." - Proverbs 29:11*

Anytime I read Proverbs 10:19 I often remember my granny. We tend to have a lot of visitors at our house when I was growing up - in particular Papa T. Papa T could talk till day-break - even when you (the listeners) are falling asleep. Sometimes if granny was around, she will send him home quoting this passage and we children tend to find it so funny. Notwithstanding, Papa T would be at our house within 3 days. He had got his own family but he just enjoys going out to talk to his friends sharing community news (gossip). You can imagine how many secrets Papa T would have passed from one family to another.

Bringing it home, how many of us have talked so much that we ended up asking God to forgive us because we had gone too far in our conversation - in not glorifying Him or in making good use of our time and thus revealing much information than necessary? Have you also noticed people who will deliberately come to engage you in conversation just to hear what you have to say? Before you know it, news have travelled round about what you said and there you are trying to remember when you said it! I am not condemning talking to people and being friendly, everything has its place, we've got to be good stewards of our time.

There is something I have observed in the life of people, both young and old and of every race, people who talks too much tend to get into a lot of relationship troubles. Everybody knows their business and they try to know everybody's business. They end up not having any business because they spend their time busying themselves about other people's businesses.

We need to know how much to say when dealing with people at work, sometime people think the more they say, the more they can impress people but often times, too much can be annoying and be of no value. Repeating yourself over and over in a meeting can become irritating to those listening. You need to judge your audience and work within time frame of the meeting - that is why it is important to have agenda. People tend to ramble on the first 10 minutes of a 30 minutes meeting then rush the last 20 minutes and found they have not even covered the main reason for the meeting! In the end another group needs the room or one of the other participant have another appointment and they end up leaving. If there is an issue in how much to say, it is best to rehearse what you need to say and be brief about it.

## The Quality of Your Speech

What is the content of our speech remembering that being wise means manifesting the fruit of the Spirit? Are our words true, wholesome, edifying, merciful, loving? Death and life are in the power of the tongue. Do our words build up or destroys?

> *"A talebearer reveals secrets, but he who is of a faithful spirit conceals a matter." - Proverbs 11:13"*

Can we be trusted with confidential information at work or not? It is amazing how people will gravitate to you as a child of God to tell you information because you will keep their confidentiality, bosses will tell you things going on at work before it is announced to the whole establishment because they know you can keep it to yourself. Maintain your integrity of being faithful, keep confidence of people so that they can continue to trust you.

> *"Confidence in an unfaithful man in time of trouble is like a bad tooth and a foot out of joint." - Proverbs 25:19*

It is important not to get involved in office gossip as it is likely for people to relay to others your part of the conversation and not what they've said.

> *"In all labour there is profit, but idle chatter leads only to poverty." - Proverbs 14:23*

How often do we chit-chat instead of getting on with our work? We are at work to do a service which we are being paid for; if we spend all the time chatting, someday the boss may get fed up and when there is restructuring, those are the things they look for to make their decisions. You may be the *Charlie* that makes everyone laugh but if your boss does not appreciate that personality, it may get awkward when he is looking for people to *let go* during restructuring.

> *"A wholesome tongue is a tree of life, but perverseness in it breaks the spirit". - Proverbs 15:4*

As children of God, we need to be careful, at work, about the jokes we laugh at, as some carries sexual connation and flirtatious behaviour. If we laugh and joke just like the world, then what differentiates us from them? If we curse like a trooper, what is the difference between us and the world?

.

> *"An evildoer gives heed to false lips; a liar listens eagerly to a spiteful tongue." Proverbs 17:4*

> *"Excellent speech is not becoming to a fool, much less lying lips to a prince." Proverbs 17:7*

Honesty is important at work, people need to rely on us that our "yes" is "yes" and "no" is "no". Sadly at the workplace, it's amazing how many people lie; they say one thing and do another which is why we tend to ask people to confirm what they've said in writing as anyone can deny they said something!

One of the root causes of lying is the fear of reprimand, fear of *if found out, what will people say?* However, it is better to say the truth and let issues be resolved before you begin to lose your reputation as an honest person. I have known people who have lied to conceal a matter and when the truth was discovered, it left a bad taste in people's mouths as a lot of time was wasted trying to fix an issue where if we had known what went wrong in the first place a lot of time would have been saved.

It is important to be transparent when issues happen; we are not machines and we can make mistakes.

I remember a case where I inadvertently combined a wrong set of files to make a whole one. The lady checking discovered the error and alerted me, I apologized and my boss said not to worry as we were able to fix it without damaging other things then he asked how it happened. I had to retrace my steps before eventually discovering how the error occurred. I told my boss and he said it's good to know so that it doesn't repeat itself at crucial moments down the road. As a result of the issue, each time I execute that process, I double-check just to make sure it doesn't happen again and I am sure other colleagues who were aware of the matter were equally careful.

It is important to pay attention during meetings so that your contribution is in line with the group discussion and not be off track. An agenda will help to keep you on track and knowing what you want to achieve at the end of the meeting. There have been times in a meeting when somebody's reply will show the person had not been concentrating, they could have been caught off-guard and just reply without thinking.

> *"An ungodly man digs up evil, and it is on his lips like a burning fire. A perverse man sows strife, and a whisperer separates the best of friends." - Proverbs 16:27-28*

As already mentioned, watch out for people who slander and gossip as it tends to tear a team apart (Proverbs 16:27-28). There are people in the team who will argue about everything; who wants to have the last say and destroys people's reputation to make themselves look good. You need to watch out that they don't pull you in their web.

## Means of Communication at Work

As indicated above there are different means of communication at work, email, Instant Messenger (IM), WhatsApp, Skype, Text, and Facebook. You need to understand the written IT policy at work and also understand the not-so-written IT policy.

Quick conversation to clarify a point can be easily said over the IM but if it involves getting a final agreement on an issue or a change to mode of operation/procedure or policy, then by all means make sure you confirm everything via email. Some companies do not back up their IM meaning whatever anyone agrees with you via IM can be denied later.

When writing emails, understand who your recipient is, their roles and responsibilities so that you can appropriately pitch the content of the email. Remember once there is an email the recipient can copy it to someone else either now or at a later stage so before you press the send button read it again. If your company deletes email after certain time and you know you need the email, copy it somewhere else so that you can reference it later. Also in terms of knowing the subject there are times when people have asked me to copy so and so on the email, and I have asked their job function just to know who I am addressing my email to.

Use of fonts, upper case/lower case lettering, colouring etc. have different meanings to different people; so understand your audience. It's amazing how our cultural difference comes into play when writing, sometimes you find some people's email come forward as rude, aggressive and confrontational. If you don't take a deep breath and react appropriately, it can snow ball into what you don't intend, so often times, take a back step and read the content and get the core of the message.

There was a time someone wrote an email and I found it to be confrontational, I felt in my heart not to respond immediately but to wait. A few minutes later the person contacted me via IM, I found his demeanour quite different on the IM, he was friendlier so we were able to resolve the issue. I noticed this colleague tend to annoy people with his email so I just make up my mind not take an offence at his emails.

Sometimes it is better to respond individually to clarify an issue instead of copying the email to the whole wide world, as people tend to be more defensive when they see other people's name on an email. A lot can be achieved one on one and only copy when the issue is resolved except where you know the discussion to the final agreement is crucial or important. Of course we are in a rat race where everyone wants to show that they are better than the others but we don't have to behave that way. Over the years I have learnt God has always *got my back.*

There was a situation where I suggested a method of doing something and two colleagues refuted it saying my method was too long, they convinced the boss to go their own way. Emails were going back and forth, I didn't respond, I left them to iron things out, they tried the other method, it didn't work and they had to come back to the method I suggested, if I had join in in the email trail, I would have also wasted time trying to prove a point instead of getting on with other pressing activities, I left them to it genuinely hoping their method will work.

In the process of communication, seek for clarity, it is important to check if the person have understood what you have said. Sometimes bullet pointing the action points helps. The same goes the other way; if somebody tells you something and you don't understand, ask for explanation. Don't be shy as it is better that people laugh at you for asking questions again and again than for you to make a costly mistake that may take months to clean up.

There have been times I have asked someone to check things with me just to make sure I am on the right track. Admittedly, one can feel embarrassed at times but it's better to be embarrassed now and people know you'll do a good job than have the reputation for being reckless and not to be trusted. Where there is an undercurrent competition of who will finish off a task first, or there is pressure from the bosses to complete a task quickly because of aggressive timescale, I have often hinted to my bosses if I think the time given for me to complete a task is totally unrealistic. Of course one needs to take time and understand the boss; know how they react to such things and know when to tell them you cannot complete a particular task on time and explain why. I once had to take my boss through the process of how I did a particular task because I felt, from his tone, he thought I should have finished earlier. When I explained, he appreciated the extra time and said it would save them time later when it came to reporting. That is one of the reasons why it is also important to listen to co-workers even if you are the *boss man*.

Learning to say "please" and "thank you" is so important as part of your communication. I have worked under different bosses and sometimes I get embarrassed the amount of thank you some of them said to me. I often thought 'but this is the job I am being paid to do'. I have come to realize, over time, that if you want your team or co-workers to go the extra mile, do the extra hours or to help meet the deadline which at the end of the day, it is the leader's name that get mentioned when it's all good or bad, you had better learn to say "thank you".

Being courteous and respectful are paramount for any worker. During meetings, pay attention. Don't dominate the meetings; try not to force your ideas alone on others; listen to theirs too. Read in between the lines and understand body language. If people are reluctant to give you a firm answer to a question, check the point out with them later after the meeting; don't be pushy during the meeting.

Keep information simple and straightforward. Try and avoid unnecessary jargon when communicating, people switch off after some time if they can't relate to what you are saying or if you are off the point in a meeting.

Don't trash someone else's idea when they are still talking! I have been in meetings where people are all so opinionated that after the meeting you feel so drained and wonder 'what's the point'. At one meeting, each time I wanted to say something, another person will jump in; in fact it got to a point, I began laughing on the inside of me thinking *'what is their problem?'*. Eventually, the Team Lead managed to get things back in control and said "can we let Toyin say something, she has been trying to" to which everyone went quiet and I offered my suggestion which if I had spoken earlier it would have saved us all about 10-15 precious minutes!

# CHAPTER 4

# HUMILITY AT WORK

*Merriam Webster dictionary described* ***humility*** *as "freedom from pride or arrogance. A quality or state of being humble".* On the opposite end of humility is pride and one of the definitions of ***pride*** in Learners' Dictionary is *"a feeling that you are more important or better than other people".*

Pride is an attitude of the mind, it originates in the heart and manifests in behaviour. It is saying in your heart, "I am better than everybody else, I can help myself, nobody can do as well as I can". When pride is in the heart, it generates all sorts of behaviour including anger, impatience, selfishness and self-centeredness because you want things done your way. Others won't seem to be as good as you are; you will be saying "I don't need anyone else, I am my own man, and nobody can do it as well as I can". Pride can be in both the rich and the poor, illiterate and educated.

As children of God, we need to examine ourselves to make sure pride does not take root in our hearts; it is sin before God. "*A haughty look, a proud heart, And the plowing of the wicked are sin.*" – Proverbs 21:4. God has promised to exalt the humble. Matthew 23:12 says "*Whoever exalts himself will be humbled, and whoever humbles himself will be exalted*" and James 4:6 says: "*God resists the proud, but gives grace to the humble*".

Pride is subtle and it may be difficult to know the difference between being assertive at work and not allowing people to walk all over us and yet not being prideful. It is often said your attitude determines your altitude. The attitude demonstrated in a given situation determines the outcome of the situation and in a workplace, it can promote you or demote you.

***"The longer I live, the more I realize the impact of attitude on life. Attitude, to me, is more important than facts. It is more important than the past, than education, than money, than circumstances, than failures, than successes, than what other people think, say or do. It is more important than appearance, giftedness or skill. It will make or break a company... a church... a home. The remarkable thing is we have a choice every day regarding the attitude we embrace for that day. We cannot change our past... we cannot change the fact that people will act in a certain way. We cannot change the inevitable. The only thing we can do is play the one string we have, and that is our attitude... I am convinced that life is 10% what happens to me and 90% how I react to it. And so it is with you... we are in charge of our Attitudes"*** - Chuck Swindoll

In a world that is so competitive how does humility or being humble help us to excel at work without being seen as docile and timid? **There are some nuggets we can pick up in the word of God:**

1. **Don't do things out of competition or rivalry with other people.** (Philippians 2:3). In a *dog-eat-dog* world, it is very easy to become so competitive that you are doing your assignments out of competition against another person to see who can complete the tasks fastest. Often this can lead to error as you end up rushing and not paying attention to details just so that they can see you finish more task than others or that you completed the tasks faster.

   Some people are so competitive at work they want to be assigned all the tasks so they can be seen to be invaluable to the team - a way of wanting to secure their position at all others' expense. If you want to compete with people like that, you will lose your peace and other things will begin to be affected. Yet we are admonished in the word of God to do our best; Colossians 3:17 says *"whatever you do in word or deed do everything in the name of the lord... giving thanks to him."* Also we are admonished to run in order to win in 1 Corinthians 9:23-27. I believe if our motives for winning is to be the best God wants us to be, to do an excellent job, not striving to get assigned work more than the others to prove a point to our boss or to secure our position, then it is a healthy competition.

I remember a time work was being allocated to us and we were being asked how long the work will take, the pressure was to give a time that will impress the boss and others. Obviously if you say you can finish at a shorter time, they can give you more. I gave a realistic time based on my experience. I found out later, a colleague who said they can finish early did not and eventually the boss had to ask someone to help him. The boss later made a comment about him that he could be over-ambitious, I thought wow! Sometimes you think you are trying to impress a boss or your colleagues; whereas they have a different opinion about you. It is better to be known that you can complete your task well to high degree of accuracy than be known to rush with all sorts of mistakes that after some time the very people you are trying to impress will take the tasks off you - most especially if you are in an industry requiring a high degree of accuracy!

Rachel and Leah were rivals, married unfortunately to the same man – a scheme devised by their father in Genesis 29. They were forever in competition who will get Jacob's attention, Leah thought it was by having lots of children, yet Jacob did not turn his attention to her. It got to a point she had to finally turn her heart to God. Rachel too tried all sorts of tricks but in the end, God had mercy on her and opened her womb. When we want to excel at work as children of God, we can't be competitive like those who do not know God. Our confidence and trust should be in God; He will make a way where there seems to be no way.

During one of the projects I worked on, there was so much scrambling of work because they were shedding-off staff and it happened that the more you are engaged in during the cut, the less likely they will get rid of you. Oftentimes, without saying a word, the boss will call me and ask me to take on some tasks without me pushing or scrambling for it. It has taught me over the years to just trust in the Lord; the Lord is *my portion in the land of the living* (Psalms 142:5).

> *"Do nothing from rivalry or conceit, but in humility count others more significant than yourselves. Let each of you look not only to his own interests, but also to the interests of others." - Philippians 2:3*

2. **Don't do things to make yourself look better and others look bad.** Don't make other people look stupid so that they can think *you are it.* Colossians 3:23 says *"whatever you do, work heartily as unto the lord and not unto men".* There is a great temptation when you have grace in a particular area and God has blessed you with intelligence in a certain area to do things just to show off your skills rather than doing it with a pure heart; not with a motive of showing off. For example, if you have been asked to do a report, during your presentation you highlighted the key points of the report then make references to why other people's report are not so good and why yours is better than theirs.

I once overheard two colleagues talking, one was highlighting a coding technique in his program but instead of leaving it there, he started talking about another person's codes and making fun of that person. I was new to IT then and was quite surprised, I felt 'does that mean when I am also out of the room that is how they make fun of my code?' Don't make fun of other people's mistakes – it could be you next time, no one is infallible

3. **Value other people's input in the team.** It is important to value other people's input in getting the job done. Being able to value other's people input requires one to list all the necessary tasks needed to get to the finishing line and realize that if at any time one of the variables is missing then the work will not be finished adequately.

   If you are an accountant and people praise you for always presenting the annual financial report accurately and on time, you need to appreciate other people's input like the bookkeeper/data entry who input every record in the spreadsheet. If they enter the wrong data, then the financial report will be wrong; which will not go down well with the management team. The admin staff who supports the team with email and tracking that everyone is doing what they are meant to be doing on time are valuable. The other colleagues chasing the invoices to establish what to enter into the system, are also valuable. When you realize other people's input and that you can't do without them you will be humble.

   1 Corinthians 12:22-26 says *"But now indeed there are many members, yet one body. And the eye cannot say to the hand, "I have no need of you"; nor again the head to the feet, "I have no need of you."* Philippians 2:3 says *"Let nothing be done through selfish ambition or conceit, but in lowliness of mind let each esteem others better than himself".*

Be considerate with junior staff as you never know one day the tables might turn. A friend of mine had a horrible experience at work, her work was being undervalued despite all her best effort. She would do all the work but when it came to the presentation, her boss never credited her for any of her input. She was overlooked for promotion but eventually she left and got another job - a more senior role. She was occupying a position where they have to approve contracts. Lo and behold, her previous boss came soliciting for the contract on behalf of her previous company. Can you imagine this lady interviewing her previous boss? She had the power to decide who the contract should go to - based on the figures etc. Unfortunately there were some irregularities in the bid from her previous company and they were not awarded the contract. These were the irregularities my friend would have been able to spot and fix before the company went out to tender but because her boss never valued her contributions, it cost the company a valuable contract.

4. **Know your strength and abilities. Don't overate yourself.** Galatians 6:3-4 say *"For if anyone thinks himself to be something, when he is nothing, he deceives himself. But let each one examine his own work, and then he will have rejoicing in himself alone, and not in another."* We have been uniquely wired and gifted. It is important to understand your strengths and abilities. Don't take on something you can't do just because it looks good on paper.

   There are people who are determined to be in a particular position yet they are not wired for it and not inclined that way. I believe it is better to be a in a position where you can establish and become an expert than in another role, where you are not performing and you end up depressed and not going anywhere. We spend too much of our time at work to end up being miserable in a particular position just because it pays well or it looks good. People will respect you more for knowing you can deliver appropriately at any given time. I know there are times we need to learn and find our feet in a particular industry not just quit because the going is tough. I remember when I newly went into IT, it was hard going initially but I found that the Lord always gives me grace to solve different issues and eventually the Lord brought me to a niche area which I have remained a better part of 15 years.

5. **Don't keep going over and over your accomplishment – don't sing your praises**. Have you been in a board room where one person is so vocal saying they've done this or that. Yes, everybody knows but it is amazing how they keep going on and on. This can become irritating at work to keep repeating that you got 1st class from Oxford or Cambridge when the people around you did not probably go to university yet by work or chance they are now in the same position as you and earning the same salary! Even if you are a top notch and keep referring to your accomplishments, after some time people will start avoiding you because they know in no time you will start bragging about your accomplishments.

   Let others sing your praises. Believe me, this world can be ruthless; they will set you up and give you a task so that you can fail and they will laugh in the end; so one needs to be careful. Let your work do the talking (Proverbs 31:31b – *"... And let her own works praise her in the gates").* Of course if you go for an interview and they ask about you and what you have done, then do tell them. Sometimes in board meeting they will ask for people's background so that people will know who they are dealing with. If you are not the first one to speak, listen to others and see how much information they are giving and speak appropriately, if people are only giving their names, how long they've been in the company and a one or 2 lines statement of your background, limit yourself to the same.

# CHAPTER 5

# HANDLING CRITICISM AND COUNSEL

**To be able to excel at work you need to be able to handle criticism and listen to counsel.**

Many people go through appraisal at work either annually/bi-annually or after a major project is completed. It is a time when the boss gives a performance review of the employee whether good or bad; giving the employee an opportunity to respond and agree to action points on the way forward. Handling this situation is critical to succeeding and excelling at work.

Nothing is 100% perfect and we live in a society where organisations are being appraised by regulatory bodies to check services are being provided according to standards. Some companies take it upon themselves to ask for feedback after you have used their services so that they can improve their services. We therefore need to be open to being appraised and welcome that opportunity to get some feedback on the services we are rendering at work and see how we can improve.

We tend to enjoy the part of being praised but being criticised is not so palatable but if we are going to improve in life, we need to listen and take on board the criticism. Correction is never easy for anybody yet the bible admonishes us that poverty and destruction comes to the one who hates correction.

*"Whoever loves instruction loves knowledge but he who hates correction is stupid. How blunt do you want it." Pro12:1*

*"Poverty and shame will come to him who disdains correction, but he who regards a rebuke will be honoured". Proverbs 13:18*

*"Rebuke is more effective for a wise man than a hundred blows on a fool." - Proverbs 17:10*

*"Strike a scoffer, and the simple will become wary; Rebuke one who has understanding, and he will discern knowledge" Proverbs 19:25*

*"He who is often rebuked, and hardens his neck, Will suddenly be destroyed, and that without remedy." - Proverbs 29:1*

*"A wise son heeds his father's instruction, but a scoffer does not listen to rebuke." - Proverbs13:1*

If you hate being corrected you'll never learn. You'll keep repeating the same mistake over and over because you are not learning from your experiences and just like in a classroom if you don't pass a paper you'll keep retaking it until you pass -if you need that subject to complete your degree.

We need to heed the corrections at work and improve so that we can succeed to the next class and excel.

I was on a particular project where I had to do a daily report, I spent a long time on the first report, after few days, my boss gave me a feedback, as much as they liked the report, it needed improvement. I was initially disappointed because he had input in the initial report and I felt it was done to specification. I had to quickly snap out of self-pity as at the end of the day, the report was not only going to him but to other managers and he had a right to change anything he wanted. I was being paid for the job and I knew 1 should not take things personally. I amended the report and we spent another 2 weeks changing things. Eventually we got it to a stable point, the report was used daily for almost a year before I moved on to another task.

My skill set improved as a result of the time spent fixing the report and in fact when I was passing the knowledge to the new person that would take over, the person was extremely impressed. Truthfully, if I was disgruntled and had made life difficult for my boss in not approaching the criticism right, I would have lost out. They might even have taken the report from me long time for having a bad attitude.

> *"A wise man will hear and increase learning, and a man of understanding will attain wise counsel." - Proverbs 1:5*

> *"Listen to counsel and receive instruction, that you may be wise in your latter days." - Proverbs 19:20*

> *"Where there is no counsel, the people fall; but in the multitude of counsellors there is safety. No man is an island." - Proverbs 11:14*

> *"A wise man is strong, yes, a man of knowledge increases strength; for by wise counsel you will wage your own war, And in a multitude of counsellors there is safety." - Proverbs 24:5-6*

It is important to make the person giving you appraisal or feedback comfortable to let you know what they have in mind and consider their action points for improvement. It's amazing how much knowledge you gain in reviews.

One of the companies I worked for did a lot of peer-to-peer review. In as much you can be embarrassed when a colleague is shredding your work to bits, you feel more confident when the work gets to the point of acceptance because the two of you had opportunity to rigorously check the work. Two heads are better than one.

Apart from handling criticism well, it is equally important to hear and listen to instruction well. When a task is being given and boss is saying how he wants things done, are you listening to the instructions or are you already planning how it should be done rather than wait for how he wants this specific task to be done?

A wise person that want to excel is someone who listens and pays attention to instructions. How many times have we done the wrong thing because we did not obey simple instructions? Not carrying out a task as required is usually because we did not listen to instructions properly. We were half-listening or we had our own preconceived ideas and then we went and did the wrong thing. As a parent and a former high school teacher, you notice that children that are calmer and obedient in class tend to do well as opposed those who may be equally intelligent but because they would not settle down in class, they missed part of what the Teacher was saying and they end up submitting sub-standard projects. They would not take time to listen to instructions, they were just waiting for the bell to go so that they can go and play with their friends.

This can happen to us at work if the boss wants us to do a task we had done before but in a different manner. We rush ahead missing the details of the new method and the boss' instruction. We need to ask for clarification if we are not sure of something. Write things down and get confirmation. Better still, ask again!

There are times when, God is also trying to pass a message across to us during our quiet times or through friends or in church, but we are too engrossed in our own way of doing things that we miss His voice on the subject matter. It is time we took stock of our lives by looking at the many mistakes we have made that could be avoided just because we did not listen to instructions. This is not limited to us listening to the one above us i.e. wives listening to their husbands, children to parents, church members to pastors but we also need to listen to the ones we are responsible for i.e. husbands listening to their wives, pastors listening to their congregation, parent listening to children, managers to their employees. God will use the foolish things to confound the wise. I have been encouraged by the wisdom that comes from younger ones who, so to say, know what is happening in the world.

There had been times I needed to buy some things and the younger ones knew more about the items, so I asked them. Pastors, you have people in your congregation much more knowledgeable about some things in your church than you are; ask them. It is nothing to be ashamed of. You are still the man/woman of God in the house but God has equipped the saints to serve as well for the extension of His kingdom here on earth.

I am in no way undermining the spiritual hierarchy in the church or home or at work. It is paramount and there is no dispute there; God has placed people in authority as a covering yet wisdom from God is not based on age but how yielded you are to the word and instructions of the Lord.

David the king listened to counsel from Abigail in 1 Samuel 25 when David was threatening to wipe out all the males in Nabal's household because Nabal refused to give David's men bread - after David had protected Nabal and his men. One of Nabal's young men got wind of what was going on and went to report to Abigail – Nabal's wife. The servant couldn't go to Nabal because everyone knew he would not listen. May we not get to the situation in our lives where we are no longer approachable to people, knowing it will only lead to argument and nothing good will be achieved.

> *"He who corrects a scoffer gets shame for himself, and he who rebukes a wicked man only harms himself. Do not correct a scoffer, lest he hate you; Rebuke a wise man, and he will love you. Give instruction to a wise man, and he will be still wiser; Teach a just man, and he will increase in learning." - Proverbs 9:7-9*

Abigail persuaded David not to carry out his threat but let God fight for him. David listened to her and changed his mind. He listened to counsel from a woman. Abigail admonished him to leave things in the hands of the Lord. Sometime later, Nabal died of heart failure without David having *blood on his hand.*

There was another time, however, that David would not listen to the commander of his army and it cost him dearly. In 2 Samuel 24, David asked Joab the commander of the army to go and count the people. In verse 3, Joab advised against this but in verse 4 we read *"Nevertheless the king's word prevailed against Joab and against the captains of the army. ...".* They went out to count despite warning David. He would not listen. It was only after he had finished counting did his heart condemn him but he had to face the music. 70,000 men died. Sometimes the devil will blind us and it appears what we are doing is absolutely correct. Even when everyone is advising against it, it is until the deed is done and the devil withdraws that our eyes now open. But, alas, it is too late. We thank God for His mercy and forgiveness but oftentimes we still have to bear the consequences of our actions.

There are also criticism and counsel that can be detriment to your career. These are criticisms and advice that are actually given to cause you harm rather than good. So it is important to *weigh the spirit*. I have heard of people being biased during appraisal out of spite and envy to discourage and bully another person out of their job.

When you notice that this is happening, even though it is hurting and causing you sadness, you need to compose yourself and try and ask the appraiser to give you examples of their comments and action points of how things can be improved. If examples and actions points are not forthcoming then you need to ask if the meeting can be rescheduled to when he can give you examples. As painful as the experience may be, getting angry and *flying off the handle* will not serve any purpose.
If some examples are given, take them on board objectively to see if there are any elements of truth in them and ask for line of action for improvement and training.

## Mentoring For Progress

The Merriam-Webster defines a **mentor** as *"a trusted counsellor or guide"*. The main job of a mentor is to guide and help the mentee achieve his/her set goals. A mentor is usually older and/or more experienced than the mentee. Mentors have usually walked through similar paths as the mentees; they have made their mistakes and know what works and what does not. Their desire is to help the mentee avoid similar pitfalls and help them start out in life in the right direction. Mentors will be more objective than friends. Friends will tell you what you want to hear so as not to hurt your feelings whilst Mentors will tell you the truth including what you do not like to hear. Mentor's job is to encourage and build the mentee at the same time be objective because he/she is not wrapped up in the emotions of the ordeal.

PAUL said to TIMOTHY you have many instructors but one father (1 Corinthians 4:15). Paul poured his life into Timothy for Timothy to become an effective minister.

NAOMI mentored RUTH for Ruth to become the wife of Boaz in the lineage of Jesus.

ESTHER was mentored by MORDECAI for her to become a queen and be instrumental in the deliverance of Jews from the death penalty engineered by Haman.

ELISHA was mentored by ELIJAH to the very end to obtain a double portion of anointing. He ended performing double the amount of miracles Elijah did.

My advice for anyone starting off in a new profession or career is to seek out someone they can be accountable to, who can help guide them along the way. I also have accountability partners who I pray with concerning our careers and we encourage one another during various challenges.

# CHAPTER 6

# WORK CULTURE

**Culture** is defined in the dictionary as *"the set of shared attitudes, values, goals, and practices that characterizes an institution or organization"*.

Understanding the culture of where you work is important. Just like each country have their traditions, culture and languages, so do different companies have their own business culture. The culture of the workplace tend to vary from country to country - even if you work for the same international company.

## Forms of Greeting

Some companies call their bosses by their titles, Mr or Ms '*Smith*' whilst some call their bosses by their first name. If you work in London where they call each other by their first names but you get moved to another country where they address their bosses by their titles, it serves you well to adopt the local culture in the office. Usually the HR would have briefed the individual being transferred of the protocol.

## Dressing

Some companies do business casual on Monday to Thursday and dress down on Friday whilst some are casual throughout, find out at interview the mode of dressing so you don't overdress or underdress. There are also different dress codes depending on your profession. Expectation for city finance workers is to dress formally. Those in catering industry are expected to have their hair tied back or pin up so that hair doesn't get into the food or drink.

Some countries allow international apparel at work but some don't, be observant not to draw attention to yourself because you want to make a statement of where you come from. Some companies may be specific on dress code when you are going on short business trips depending on the environment.

I remember one time we were going to a branch office in USA, a bit remote; during the briefing, we were told as ladies not to wear strings or short skirts, told not to wear open shoes etc. I was surprised how specific they were, though not strange to me as we've been admonished in the word of God to be modest in our dressing. On getting to the site, we soon realize the reason for the specifics in dressing. The office is remote, and also located in cabin near a factory with 99% men, also most of the ground is all pebble. Even though it was super-hot, weather wise, we saw the sense in being asked to dress modestly.

## Start and Leaving Time

Before leaving office, observe and understand what goes on. Do people leave exactly at 5pm after doing 8hrs or people leave when work is completed? I have known people who were so strict on their 40hours a week and they are not flexible to wait extra hours, managers have taken notice and made comments, so and so will not stay behind, please pass the work to Mr X. I am not suggesting you work yourself to the ground or become a man pleaser and just be hanging around late in the office for the sake of it; basically understand and observe what is going on. I worked at a company where by 5.30pm the place is completely deserted in fact if the boss sees you in the office around 5.30pm, he tends to ask "don't you have a home to go to?" The business culture was strictly a 9 to 5.30; furthermore, to stay beyond 6pm, the boss will have to email security to alert them.

I have equally worked for other companies where they see 10hrs a day as normal at no extra pay. Of course anything over 10hours should be brought up to the manager to see if this is a common thing and if there is any plan for overtime. I remember a company I worked for, where because it was awkward to get to town after 5.30, one of my colleagues kicked a fuss for the team being repeatedly delayed almost every day. Eventually the boss met with management and it was decided that definitely 10-11 hours work was needed to meet the schedule and the management agreed to 6 days' pay for 5 days' work to compensate. Everyone was happy including those of us who were not bold enough to tackle the matter head on.

## Usage of Phones and Social Media

Read your IT policy handbook regarding usage of phones and social media. I have known contractors whose contracts were not extended because the log showed they were on line a lot, which the company interpreted as they were not busy.

Some companies frown upon use of Facebook, twitter etc at work. Some people's online comment on the Facebook have led to disciplinary issues because one of the people on their contact' list felt the comment posted online was about them and sued for harassment.

Some people do not allow phones at the desk, even at one company, you are not allowed to speak on the stairs! Each company have its own policy. As most offices are open plan, taking calls in your own foreign language talking with higher tone will draw attention. I know one guy who is forever on the phone and you have to tap him to draw attention to him, of course he did not last on the job. Keep your phone on silence not vibration or ringer, it could embarrass you in meetings.

## Lunch Time and Where to Eat

How long do people take lunch and at what time? Can you eat at your desk or is this frowned upon? Is it ok to eat fish and chips in the open plan office? Study your environment and act appropriately.

## Holiday Time

Taking holidays even when you are entitled to it at wrong time can leave a bad taste in Management's mouth. Try and find a suitable time within project timelines; someone taking leave during critical time of the project looks bad from the Team Lead's point of view. Try and take your holidays as it is important for refreshment purposes and the managers knows holidays are crucial but take it with the consent of bosses. There is no sense in asking your boss after seeing the holiday on the cheap online, paid for it and then coming to request for time-off only to be turned down and then you get seriously disappointed.

## Teamwork

Observe if the team work together nicely or are they competitive. How would you handle it if you being a helpful person wanting to mock in, see that the team wins but you notice everyone else takes credit for your work? You need to step back and see how you can map out how your work will be identified. Is there a tracker where you log who did what? If you are asked to work with someone and find they always take credit for the work, you might ask them to share the presentation so both of you have opportunity to present different segments of the work.

One of the projects I did, the boss realized what was going on and actually created sub trackers to record each input to the project as some people are not transparent enough to let people know who contributed to the work. Try and be cooperative when working with others, **cooperation destroys competition and eliminates pride**. More have been discussed in chapter 4.

## Relationships at Work

> *"A man who has friends must himself be friendly"* - *Proverbs 18:24a*

Be friendly and courteous at work. You are not an island, we need each other, smile and greet people. In the circle of friends you will know who to really be close to and that is where you need wisdom and discernment.

Proverbs 12:26 says "*a righteous man choose his friends carefully*". Many lives have been ruined or blessed by the types of friends they have. You need to ask yourself questions like: does this person who I spend most of my time with lead me to God or take me away from God? Forming relationships at work needs careful thought. The person you go to lunch with day in day out, who are they? Do they sit to crucify everyone in the team and then go and spread what you've equally shared to others? *"Do not be deceived; "Evil company ruins good habits" 1 Corinthians 15:33.*

What are their values? What do they stand for? "*He who walks with wise men will be wise, but the companion of fools will be destroyed.*" - Proverbs 13:20. If you stay long in the company of wise people you will become wise.

> *"Make no friendship with an angry man, and with a furious man do not go, lest you learn his ways and set a snare for your soul." - Proverbs 22:24-25*

> *"When wisdom enters your heart and knowledge is pleasant to your soul. Discretion will preserve you and understanding will keep you. To deliver you from; the evil man who speaks perverse things those who walk in the ways of darkness those who rejoice in doing evil those whose ways are crooked and devious in their paths the immoral woman the seductress who flatters with her words who forsakes the companion of her youth and forgets the covenant of her God." - Proverbs 2:10-12*

By their fruits you shall know them. When you start operating in wisdom and discernment, you'll be able to know who people are and decide not to meddle with them. Joseph, endowed with wisdom, when confronted with a seductive and adulterous woman, did not toy with her or try to reason with her, he fled; that is wisdom. A woman like that does not listen to reason. 1 Thessalonians says *"Flee every appearance of evil ..."*

So many affairs have started innocently at work places. Lunch time rendezvous' and after work clubbing before going home. If you don't have your standard set in your spirit, it is so easy to compromise so that you can fit in. You have to have the two letter word NO ready when you don't want to go anywhere you don't feel like. They may make fun of you initially eventually they will accept you for who you are and even let others know.

When we have office parties, my team specifically ask which fruit juice they should order because they know what I think of drinking alcohol. I don't need to defend myself, my conviction is my conviction. Sometimes we Christians try to shy away from our convictions when other faith do not make any apologies of their beliefs and demand stuff in accordance to their religion.

I have enjoyed my time at work and still keep in touch with some friends long after leaving the workplace but not at the detriment of my faith. God has also opened door for me to share my faith and what I believe. I can recall many times, work schedule will be rearranged in the work place to allow me time to serve God on Sunday.

In fact it is always interesting when they ask me what my husband does and I say "a minister"; they can't reconcile a vicar's wife being in the work place. Those interesting conversations tend to give me opportunities to share the gospel. The Lord has always granted me favour in being able to take time out to attend Sunday service when we are meant to be in the office, I leave at a certain time and come back to the office and to the glory of God manage to do my work on schedule.

One day we were in USA for a project from UK on a three weeks' stint – that's two Sunday away from home! I met a Christian on site, who agreed to give me a ride to a church on Sunday morning. I was waiting at the hotel foyer, this guy didn't show up and he didn't have my UK phone number, he called my boss to say he couldn't make it and they should pass the message to me. Lo and behold, I saw my boss at the foyer requesting that she will go and drop me at the church; on top of that, she said I should call her when I was done so she could come and pick me up! She didn't, however have to do that as I made friends with some people at the church who were able to drop me back to the hotel. These new friends even came to pick me again during the week for an evening meal. My colleagues at work were shocked how could we have become friends by meeting just one time, it was a testament of Christians being united in one spirit no matter where you come from or how many times you've met someone before.

## CHAPTER 7

# DECIDING WHEN TO CHANGE JOBS

The idea of being in the same job for life has almost disappeared as indicated in a job-for-life article by LV.COM. It is rare these days to meet anyone who has been in the same company throughout their working career and if you do, they will have moved departments within the same company

> *"The research from retirement specialist LV= marks a sharp shift from past generations, with today's younger workers set to have twice as many jobs as their grandparents, with the 'job for life' virtually extinct (2). The typical Briton entering the workforce today can expect to have nine jobs including one major career change across 48 years of working (1). Today's new workers also faces a significantly longer working life, retiring seven years later than their grandparents did (66 vs. 59) (3) with nearly a quarter (23%) working well into their 70s. More than half (55%) can also expect to be made redundant at least once across their 48 working years (18-66).* (https://www.lv.com/about-us/press/article/job-for-life)

Peter Capaldi during his interview, when he stepped down from Dr Who, said "Three years is the maximum length of time anyone should stay in a job" "I've never done one job for three years. This is the first time I've done this and I feel it's time for me to move on to different challenges," he said. (http://www.bbc.co.uk/news/business-38828581)

Industry expectation varies how long it's sensible for people to stay in a job before moving under normal circumstance. The webpage http://www.jobsite.co.uk/worklife/moving-jobs-how-often-19931/ contained comments from business experts

> *"Sue Honoré is at Ashridge, one of the world's leading business schools, which has researched this subject. She says: "If you can show that each move is a progression, then it is fine." However, she adds: "In crude terms, employers do not want to invest in someone who does not give them a return on investment. It is not just the financial cost of hiring and training someone but also the time and effort put in…"*

> *"Zoe Fowler, a Director at recruitment specialist Cordant People, says: "If, for example, you've had four jobs in four years, that may portray you as someone who gets restless and bored easily and that would probably make an employer cautious in interviewing or hiring you."*

> *"Sue agrees: "Our research shows that employers accept job moves with a two-year gap, although they want good people to stay longer."*

> *"And Kaz adds: "Changing jobs simply to earn more money is not always a good idea; the most important factor of a job is whether or not it gives you satisfaction.*

*The best kind of change is to a job that makes you happy."*

*"Karen Meager is a Career Coach and works with Monkey Puzzle Training & Consultancy. She says: "Fast-moving tech industries are much more comfortable with people moving frequently, whereas industries with a longer product lifecycle, like engineering, value people who stick around longer."*

*"Sue adds: "Changes out of your control are fine – a family house move, redundancy, on good terms with the employer, and so forth."*

Aldi carried out a survey of 1000 people examining why people want to change job and found that money was the major factor, with failing to land pay rises the most commonly cited answer, followed by office politics and then poor morale (http://www.telegraph.co.uk/finance/jobs/11287241/Sick-of-your-job-Heres-why-people-want-to-change-career.html)

**Before changing job, it is important to analyse why you want to change job and see if the need to change can be met at your current job.**

The next few pages contain my views on the reasons why people changed jobs in the survey carried by Aldi:

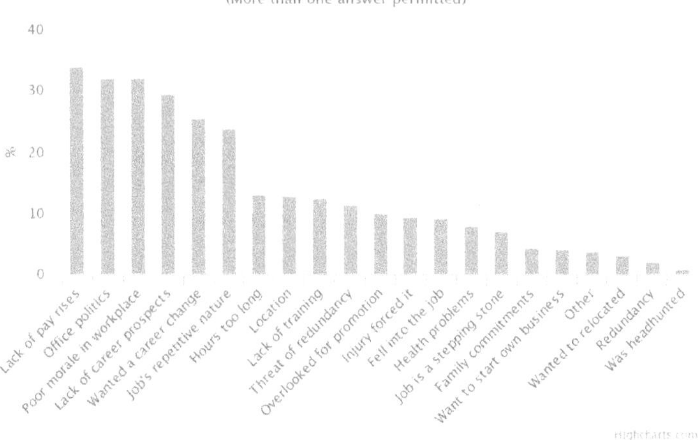


**A. Lack of pay rise**

Usually a job role (permanent job) will have a salary band where you negotiate your starting point when you commence the job and annually or at review, there is a discussion of being moved to the next level. Sometimes moving from one band to another is automatic whereas some companies depend on the performance and increment is only approved with a performance score of above average.

If you have reached a plateau where there is no salary increment due to performance issue, then before you resign, ask your boss what you need to do to improve your performance. If you leave with under performance, it may reflect on your reference, the underperformance may also highlight that maybe you are not really suited for the role. Could you ask to be moved to another role whereby your skills set is suitably matched and if your performance improve then salary might be better?

If you have reached plateau of the salary band, check with the boss what you need to do to move to the higher band. I have known people who through undergoing a training/exams etc., have been moved up a salary band.

For contractors, sometimes negotiating pay rises can be tricky. I have known people who have asked for increase in pay and their contracts were not renewed. I have known those who have asked and they got the increase in pay but their contracts were not renewed. I have known those who have asked and they got the increase in pay and their contracts were not renewed. I have known those who have asked and they have got the increase. You need to *test the waters* before asking - basically pray. The heart of kings is in God's hands and a worker is worthy of its wages.

There was a time, after one year on a contract, I asked for an increase during renewal, the agent said "no"; he didn't think the employer will give as they were cutting staff but I felt my responsibility had increased. I was even negotiating for the agent to reduce his commission, but he said "no", their commission was standard. 6 months after, I felt compelled again, lo and behold, I was granted an increment of 6%. Talk of timing, not long after the increment was approved, unfortunately the agent who runs the small recruitment firm died. If I had accepted "no" and never brought the issue up again, I may never have gotten the increase. So go with the flow, if you feel led to ask, do and trust God for favour.

**B. Poor morale in the workplace.**

You can see from the chart above, poor morale is high as one of the reasons that people change jobs. Proverbs 17:1 (NLT) says *"Better a dry crust eaten in peace than a house filled with feasting--and conflict".*

We spend more time at work than at home so to be at work where morale is low is hard work. Poor morale can be triggered by different reasons – work not recognized, macro management of staff, bullying behaviours, poor work conditions, less reward systems, negative attitude from team members

Pray before you leave as God might want to use you as an agent of change where you are. There was dissention in the camp in Acts 6 but after prayers, God granted the apostles wisdom what to do to facilitate change. If you don't feel led to approach the boss, God can still use you, by you being at peace in yourself and positive at work may help boost the morale of team members.

I was in a team once whereby morale was low, my team became well-known because everything that could go wrong did. New management, new software, new ways of working, all being implemented at the same time; we also worked long hours. Each day was moan, moan. One day I felt *'no, this is not normal, God of peace and order is my God'.* So I started to pray and also shared with my prayer partners, over the months, changes started to happen including the company changing the leader. Eventually we reached our end goals albeit with so much pressure and long hours but we got there in the end. If I had left earlier, I would have missed the opportunity of seeing God at work. Also my encounter with the new manager opened more doors for me at that establishment. So just because things are *hot* does not mean it is time to quit, weigh it in the spirit before changing jobs due to low morale.

At another time, I was at a company and again due to changes of ways of working and political unrest in some of the countries we were assisting, I felt to apply for a job that came up in another company which is much closer to home with extra pay and expense paid. Four of my colleagues also applied. I was offered the job and now was struggling on how to let my boss know as I had only been in the role 7 months; and my contract was just extended for another six months with a month's notice period. I just felt it was ok to accept the offer even though after I had accepted the offer, I was feeling bad thinking 'I hope I had done the right thing'. Feeling apprehensive, I eventually told my boss and handed in my notice, not sure of what his response will be.

I really don't like letting people down and he did make me feel bad initially when I told him as I was a key player for a particular product but eventually he was ok as I assured him I will complete my one month notice which in IT contract some agents might put pressure on you to start early so that they can securely know you had started on the new site but the new agent and company agreed to wait.

By the time my notice period was up and by God's grace, I had completed all hand over documentation which made my boss very happy, on my last day he took us to lunch and saw me off right to the gate and even said if you are not happy where you are going, make sure you call me and we will sort out a role for you here. Lo and behold 3 weeks after, I got a text from one of my previous colleagues asking if I was aware before I left that the project was going to be capped. I said "no". Apparently after I left, because of continuous political unrest in one of the countries we were implementing, the company decided to shelve all projects which meant our services were no longer required till further notice. Looking back now, God, who knows the end from the beginning (Isaiah 46:10), knew that it was time for me to leave before I got caught up in the fiasco. Indeed His eyes run to and from the earth showing Himself strong and behalf of those whose heart is loyal to Him (2 Chronicles 16:9). If I had not taken the opportunity that opened up, I am not sure what would have happened. I was on the new contract for 15 months with lots of opportunities to work from home, it was one of the best companies I worked for. So again, pray and see how the Lord is leading you and move appropriately.

C. **Wanted a career change / Want to start your own business**

Sometimes you just come to point in life when you simply want a change; you want to try something new. Before changing, do research about your self – skills, talents and abilities. There are lots of analysis tools available for use online or you can check www.freshstartmentoring.com.

In my 30+ years of working I have changed career 3 times from the time I left university in 1984. I did an Electrical Engineering degree and worked for the civil service for almost 8 years as an engineer. I enjoyed the job but was not really fulfilled. With a growing family and ministry, I felt I needed a career that will allow me to combine work and motherhood. I prayed and felt led to move into teaching, it meant going back to school for a year to do teachers training. Surviving on a teachers training bursary would have been much tougher financially but the redundancy package from my employer helped cushioned the training bursary shortfall.

Moving into education, teaching a subject that I love and seeing lives changed made me enjoy the transition and the Lord opened doors immediately I finished the training – a school that was 15 minutes' drive close to home. It gave me opportunity to have the same school holidays with the children and able to understand what is going on with their education. On top of this, I was able to set up supplementary Saturday school in Maths and English. The downside of teaching was the out of hours marking; maths being a compulsory subject for all students, you can bet you have full marking like the English and science teachers. So evening hours was taking up marking once the kids go to bed.

As time went on, we moved to another country which required if I was going to continue teaching, I will need another training and start at the bottom of scale. Changing from engineering to teaching previous years saw my pay cut down by almost 35%, I honestly do not have the motivation to do this again in another country plus studying again whilst starting a new ministry plus 3 kids, after much prayers I felt led to go into IT. Do something where there is no more working after office hours.

The interesting part in all these is that all my career changes were an off shoot of what I had enjoyed doing even in my first job or that which I had a natural inclination for - mathematics. It was a matter of the Lord saying "what do you have in your hands?" My IT career have panned over 19years and I have been in a particular area for almost 15 years. During this time, I have worked with at least 14 companies with contracts ranging from 3 weeks to 3years. I'm saying all these to affirm that the career path and length of each person is unique, nothing is the same. How God leads each person is different. The key thing is to be prayerful, do your research, seek counsel and seek to glorify God in all your decisions. God has wired you with unique skills and abilities and His desire is that you be fulfilled in the job. It is tough being in a job for a long time and not enjoying the job, so do your research. (Visit FreshStartMentoring.com for the career analysis tools.) Even when you miss it, don't get bogged-down and think that is the end, dust yourself up and try again.

D. **Hours too long**

We live in an age where work life balance is being skewed. Managers are demanding more from employees and not many people can still say they work only 8 hours a day.

If you are getting to where you can't handle the long hours, check if you can do part time or check if you can work from home to cut out the stress of commuting. Some companies are now championing good work-life balance and it's beginning to gain grounds. If you are not able to achieve it then it may be a good time to consider changing the job but make sure you research into the new company and ask question before jumping ships because sometime long hours is just the nature of some jobs and you have to decide maybe instead of changing the job, it might calls for changing career! If you are a nurse, then long hours are part of it; as a teacher, long hours in the evenings is the order of the day during school days. The finance industry tend to work long hours towards the end of the month or financial-reporting periods. Instead of changing jobs what about taking a junior role with less responsibility and less pay whilst your family is growing.

E. **Lack of Training**

If you are in an organization where they are not offering training but you enjoy the company, before leaving because of no training, ask HR if they are willing to pay for training if you find one. If they say "no", check is it a "no" forever or a "no" for now.

I was in a situation when a company was introducing a new tool; as contractor, there is a belief that only permanent staff should be trained so the person putting people forward did not put my name forward even though I would have loved to learn the new tool. In a way I was initially disappointed but I quickly got over it. 6 months down the line, they wanted someone to do some basic work on the new tool, which in quote would have been too tedious for the seniors they brought into the project, so they asked if I could help. The task was mundane and for the rate I was on, it should have been given to someone much junior, I took the job on and I believed I gave it my all, they were impressed and that was what God used to secure me another year worth of work as the piece I was doing now became a core of their processes. Not long after, I was given full access to do development work on the system. I was able to learn on the job and reach a reasonable skill level. If I had left out of offence, I would have lost out. I was at the company altogether for 3 years. So before changing check and weigh your options.

F. **Overlooked for promotion**

Being overlooked for promotion can be painful when you are qualified for it or when you have worked for it in accordance to your boss promising that if you get this training done etc. you will be promoted, and then you find it was given to someone else who is not qualified or has not worked for it.

If you were interviewed for the promotion but it was given to someone else, ask for feedback. If it is obvious there is no apparent reason. Pray and seek God's direction as this might be trigger that will open your eyes to the new door God is opening. The key thing is to check your attitude when you are being overlooked, is God allowing this because He has something better for you at the current company or in a new company. He is the one who closes a door where no man can open and open a door where no can shut. Promotions comes from God not from man.

G. **Fell into the job/ Headhunted**

There are times out of the blue, a job will open up or you will be headhunted. I have situations where agencies have called me as a result of recommendation, there are times I have accepted and see it as opened door to next venture like I shared under the section of **Poor Morale in the workplace** and there are times I have turned it down. On a particular case, I got a call for a role near home (less than 1hr). I was tempted to consider it as it will mean no weekly commute but I just didn't feel like taking it. Eventually I told the agent not to bother. As I stayed longer at my current role, there were more opportunities to work from home sometime I will be home for 6 weeks which meant not commuting whether weekly or daily. It worked out ok for me to have turned down the job. Before you turned down a job you are head hunted for or that just opened up, do your research, find out as much info as possible including:

- Notice period
- Salary structure
- What is the difference between the new position and your current one in the short term and medium term
- How will it affect your family and your finances
- Above all what is God saying to you in the situation?

## H. Want To Relocate/Family Commitment

Relocation and family commitment are usually two of the main factors people change jobs. They are things that are explainable at interview when asked why you changed jobs. Hopefully you have plenty of time to prepare for the relocation or change in family commitment that is triggering the job change. The more time you have to prepare for job change the better as there are steps that can be followed to ease the job change. I had to change job once because kids were about to start their A level and O levels, I wanted time to help out with revision in the evenings, the job was like 30% pay cut but I have no regrets as it was beneficially for the family.

## I. Termination

Termination from a job can be very painful, you feel let down; at times shameful; thinking 'how can it happen to me?'

In everyone's career, there is at least one termination, which could result from business closing down, buyout, funding coming to an end or performance issue. We all want to have the choice to walk out of a job but sometimes it doesn't always happen that way. If it is through lack of performance, ask for a feedback if environment dictates. Earlier on in my IT career, I was terminated at a contract, I was gutted as I thought I was really trying my best but the feedback was I was taking long to complete my tasks and the company wanted somebody more experienced. After my tears, I had to dust myself up and applied for jobs again. I prayed and the Lord did a miracle, I got a job soon afterwards in a similar role where I was able to use what I had learnt in the previous role. The new company did not take reference and just went by me answering correctly the technical questions during the interview. I was able to do well at the interview by recalling some of the painful experiences I had in my previous job. All things worked out together for good.

If termination is due to some misdemeanour on your part, repent, dust yourself up and ask God for mercy to open another door. Proverbs 24:16a says *"For a righteous man may fall seven times and rise again"*

**Whatever the reasons may be for wanting to change jobs, <u>prepare for your exit</u>. The bible says a righteous man is not hasty.**

1. Analyse what you are looking for in your new role – type of work and responsibilities, locations, salary etc. be true to yourself.

2. Check your notice period – will the new job allow for notice period, the more senior the role you have, the longer the notice period. Some short-term contract need an immediate start!

3. Check requirements for getting your next dream job. If you need extra qualification, start doing private training before resigning or try and seek for more relevant duties in your current role to enhance your skill set.

4. Have at least the equivalent of 2 months of your salary in savings; just in case when you get to your new job things don't work out and you need to leave; at least you can be sure you can meet some of your bills whilst looking for another job!

5. Be in good standing with whom you are going to get reference from before you leave your current job.

6. On the home front, go on your family holiday if you are planning to go before starting the new job so that you are not taking time off unduly when you start a new job, however if you have booked for a holiday and an interview comes up, be transparent when asked if you have holidays coming up, some people cancel family holidays because of the need to take up the new job and then they are not able to take one for a while and the family members feel aggrieved. Employers are humans too. There was a time, I was allowed to start for a few days, go for my holidays and then come back to the new job. Trust God for favour.

7. Begin to gradually tidy up your email inbox and documents saved on the work laptop, you will be amazed how busy you are on your last day, it's as if everyone needs something before you leave and you end up forgetting to store some of your documents. Try to see the last week before your actual leaving week as your last week.

8. As you prepare your CV, think about how you will answer why you are changing jobs or why there is a frequency in changing jobs. Is it for family reasons, career progression, or job cuts etc.?
   When preparing CV don't inflate your experience or say something in your CV that you have not done, I have known people who exaggerated their experiences only to get to their new job work and when demand is placed on that skill they listed on their cv, they are found wanting. It is better to be truthful and believe God for open doors.

There was a time a recruiter called me about a job and I said I only had an overview about a particular software, he said looking at my CV though the employer was looking for more experience he felt I have enough experience in other areas to pick up quickly what was needed. On top of that, I told the guy another agent had put me forward and they had come back to say I was not shortlisted. He said he will check and come back to me. 8pm an unusual time for an agent to call a job seeker, the agent said the employer had not seen my CV, nobody had submitted my CV and he had managed to secure me an interview the following day. The Lord granted me favour at the interview and I was given the job. It was tough initially with hardly any experience on that particular software but the Lord surrounded me with good people, I was able to pick things up, spent off-days learning and by the time I left the job 8 months later to another job due to unexpected changes in domestic arrangement, I had learnt so much and forever grateful to God for that opportunity and chance given to me by the employer.

9. Despite all preparation, with conviction in your heart, you might just have to bite the bullet and resign and move on. After a short term IT training in October 1998, the common sense approach was to do some work as a supply teacher till I get the IT job I had just been recently trained for, however I felt if I went back into the teaching, I would not have time to look for work or attend interviews. Those days, I do not have the mini version of the software on my computer so I had nowhere to practice what I just learnt, so it was race against clock to secure an appointment before I forgot all that I had learnt. My action was also confirmed when I heard a man of God who came to our church preach on faith that has no back door (Bishop Makanto – October 1998). You

know when God had already spoken to you about a cause of action, where, to the eyes of the world, things do not make sense including you, then you go to church and God confirmed it through a message, you feel like jumping up shouting “that’s it!”

To this day, I can’t remember the scripture he shared, just the phrase ‘FAITH THAT HAS NO BACK DOOR’. Well, I was rejuvenated to say the least and kept on with my grind of sitting in front of the computer 9am to 5pm, for one solid month, sending out application upon application - looking for work. In return I got rejection letter upon rejection letter as I did not have the required experience. The only meaningful exposure on this software now amounted to 3 months, but I persisted, eventually I got a job, 60 miles away from home. I was desperate as by this time, bills had piled up, overdraft had been exhausted. Distance was no issue at this point. I was not a fan of the motorway but I had no choice and with the boldness of God got behind the wheels. For three good months, I did daily roundtrip from Edmonton to Cambridge till that job came to an end and I got another one 30miles from home.

10. Lastly, leave with a good reputation, you don’t know where you will meet people again. In the past 10 years at every company I have worked for I have met people I had worked with before and if I had been horrible to them, I wouldn’t have been comfortable working with them again. On many occasions, people that I knew before were instrumental to me being hired as they had recommended me after they realized I was shortlisted for interview.

# CHAPTER 8

# PROMOTION

We live in a very competitive world, gone are the days of automatic promotion to the next grade/level after being in the same role for some years so long as you get above average rating during annual appraisal. These days, there are so many things that bosses look for in getting people promoted. It is no longer the longest staff in the team that get the team lead position when it becomes vacant.

Sometimes the least person to others in terms of 'experience' may end up being the lead and everyone wonders why, not knowing the managers have been studying everyone for a long time so it is good to prepare yourself as a promotable material. Of course the word of God makes us know that promotion does not come from the east nor the west but from the father of light but I believe there are things we can learn from different characters in the bible that enhanced their chances of being promoted.

Here are some wisdom nuggets to help us excel and become promotion ready to take a higher role in the company:

## Faithfulness

The Lord Jesus shared a powerful parable in Matthew 25 to illustrate the point that promotion and progress is in the heart of God and faithfulness is one of the keys to being promoted. A business man travelling out of the city gave his 3 employees talents to trade according to their ability. The ones with 5 and 2 talents traded and made 100% profit whilst the one with 1 talent did not trade but went to hide his own because he felt his boss was a wicked man; always wanting to reap where he did not sow. On his return, the business man asked for an account; just like at the end of the year, there is an annual appraisal at the work place. The boss was excited and congratulated the 2 employees that made profit and promoted them to be rulers over more things. Matthew 25:21, 23 "***His lord said to him, 'Well done, good and faithful servant; you were faithful over a few things, I will make you ruler over many things. Enter into the joy of your lord".***

For the one who did not trade, made no gain and actually made a loss as the monetary value would have diminished from the time he was given if nothing has been done with it, he was severely rebuked and his talent was taken from him and given to the other who made a profit. Matthew 25: 29-30 "***For to everyone who has, more will be given, and he will have abundance; but from him who does not have, even what he has will be taken away. And cast the unprofitable servant into the outer darkness. There will be weeping and gnashing of teeth".***

God expect us to make progress and exercise our God-given abilities at work. Our employers expect us to use our skillsets to make contributions and add value to the success of the company. We were employed with a particular skill set and at the end of the year our productivity will be judged; if we go and hide our talents because we think our bosses are the ones who take the glory or because we are not seeing immediate monetary reward, we end up losing out. Skills not used will end up being forgotten and it will appear as if you have never had them before.

I have shared a testimony (in Chapter 7 section on lack of training) when I mentioned they gave me a task meant for a junior person, I did it with finesse and they gave me a bigger role later. The bible makes us know that God delights in the prosperity of the righteous. God is happy when we prosper; He is happy when we succeed. God is excellent in business, He gave us the gifts and He is looking for profit. People tend to frown on making money because of 1 Timothy 6:10 says "*The love of money is the root of all evil*" forgetting Ecclesiastes 10:19b says "*money answers all things*".

Having a balanced view of money is important, giving is one of the spiritual gifts which included giving financially, Paul prayed for the Philippians for them meeting his needs financially (Philippians 4:19). The women gave to the Lord Jesus out of their substance (Luke 8:3). Job was the richest man in the east yet he was described as righteous (Job 1:8). It is when you allow money to lure you away from God and compromise your faith or stand in God that it becomes a problem. The parable of the talent shows the boss was not happy at all with the servant who hid his talent.

Stay faithful and focus on your mission. People tried to distract Nehemiah several times during the building project he embarked on for God but he remained faithful and focused. (Nehemiah 4:6). Ignore the naysayers; in the end they will come to celebrate you. Don't be distracted when the going gets tough.

## Work Hard and Be Diligent

> *"The hand of the diligent will rule, but the lazy man will be put to forced labour." - Proverbs 12:24*
>
> *"Do you see a man who excels in his work? He will stand before kings; He will not stand before unknown men." - Proverbs 22:29*

*"A man's gift makes room for him, and brings him before great men." - Proverbs 18:16*

If you are diligent and hardworking, people will find you out. David was called to the kings' palace because the king requested for a skillful musician (1 Samuel 16:17-18). To become a skillful player of a musical instrument takes practice. David's gift took him to the presence of the king but he had to pay a price of daily practicing his instrument. Are you practicing the gifting God have given you? Are you updating your training? If your company does not send you for training, there are many online training free of charge. Are you comfortable to continue to be at the same level or will you deny yourself a bit of pleasure to do something different that will distinguish you from others? David was not the only instrumentalist at that time, but he was known for his skills in playing.

*So Saul said to his servants, "Provide me now a man who can play well, and bring him to me." Then one of the servants answered and said, "Look, I have seen a son of Jesse the Bethlehemite, who is skillful in playing, a mighty man of valour, a man of war, prudent in speech, and a handsome person; and the LORD is with him." - 1 Samuel 16:17-18*

It is not in the sleeping and lazing away that destiny meets with us, it is in active duty. Not just sleeping physically but we can also be sleeping at work in our attitude of being lackadaisical - not pushing ourselves to learn and hone our skills. It takes time to study, even after work, till we understand the policies and procedures required to do our job excellently

*"Do not love sleep, lest you come to poverty; Open your eyes, and you will be satisfied with bread." - "Proverbs 20:13*

> *"Laziness casts one into a deep sleep, and an idle person will suffer hunger." - Proverbs 19:15*

If you enjoy your comfort and love to sleep and be in bed all day, then be ready to be a companion of Mr Poverty. I have known people who can't but sleep 8 to 10 hours, this is alright if you have worked hard but lazy people can roll in bed and have every excuse not to work. With that attitude you'll get fired from work and bring embarrassment to yourself and your family.

> *"He who loves pleasure will be a poor man; He who loves wine and oil will not be rich." - Proverbs 21:17*

> *"The soul of a lazy man desires, and has nothing; but the soul of the diligent shall be made." - Proverbs 13:4*

The world is full of dreamers. Oh they desire this and that, yet the next morning they can't get up to go to work. Sometimes we can also spend them analysing all the theories and how things should be done but until we begin to actually do the work, it is all in the head and soon the bosses will differentiate between the talkers and the doers.

The bosses are observant and news go round among the leaders that so and so, whines and complain if given some difficult task. I know a particular colleague who, to get out of a task, will complain and shred the work to pieces saying "this is not sorted yet and that is not sorted". By the time he's done, the work is sometimes taken from him and given to others, or alternatively he will do the barest minimum. Of course he didn't last in the job. Ruth was noticed at Boaz's field for her hard work.

> *Then Boaz said to his servant who was in charge of the reapers, "Whose young woman is this?" So the servant who was in charge of the reapers answered*

> *and said, "It is the young Moabite woman who came back with Naomi from the country of Moab. And she said, 'Please let me glean and gather after the reapers among the sheaves.' So she came and has continued from morning until now, though she rested a little in the house."* - Ruth 2:5-7

It is amazing that all the people God used were busy and hardworking people. Moses at the burning bush, Elisha when he was plowing with his oxen, David in the fields shepherding the flock skilfully. *"So David shepherded them according to the integrity of his heart; and guided them with his skillful hands."* - Psalms 78:72. Rebecca as a shepherdess met Abraham's servant – who asked her for a drink but she ended up giving drink to all the camels also Genesis 24:12-18. Are you able to go the *extra mile* at work? Add a little of extra touch to that presentation, you never know who is watching. Gideon sneaked out to get food whilst others were hiding, God sent an angel to announce his next assignment.

## Servant Heart

> *"After the death of Moses the servant of the LORD, it came to pass that the LORD spoke to Joshua the son of Nun, Moses' assistant, saying: "Moses My servant is dead. Now therefore, arise, go over this Jordan, you and all this people, to the land which I am giving to them—the children of Israel. Every place that the sole of your foot will tread upon I have given you, as I said to Moses" - Joshua 1: 1-3*

After the death of Moses, God spoke to Joshua to take up the reigns of leadership. Joshua was Moses assistant, basically Moses' servant. Have you ever wondered why God did not choose Moses' children but picked Joshua? God was looking at the heart, a heart of service just like God described Moses as His servant, and God was looking for another servant. Someone that will serve Him, serve the people and lead them to the Promised Land; someone who will finish the task Moses had started. It is the same with bosses, there is something they look for when wanting to promote people. It is not how long you've been in the organization or how closely-related you are with the owner. For the progress of the company, bosses will look for who can lead the people yet with a servant heart. Joshua had served Moses well, he ran errands, he stayed where he was meant to (Exodus 24:14-15).

> *"So Moses arose with his assistant Joshua, and Moses went up to the mountain of God. And he said to the elders, "Wait here for us until we come back to you. Indeed, Aaron and Hur are with you. If any man has a difficulty, let him go to them." Then Moses went up into the mountain, and a cloud covered the mountain" - Exodus 24:14-15*

Joshua served and was obedient to Moses when asked to spy the land, he went, came back and gave a good report (Numbers 14:6-9). He didn't follow the popular opinions. He was rewarded for his service and promoted to take the place of Moses (Joshua 3:7).

> *"But Joshua the son of Nun and Caleb the son of Jephunneh, who were among those who had spied out the land, tore their clothes; and they spoke to all the congregation of the children of Israel, saying: "The land we passed through to spy out is an exceedingly good land. If the LORD delights in us, then He will bring us into this land and give it to us, 'a land which flows with milk and honey.' Only do not rebel against the LORD, nor fear the people of the land, for they are our bread; their protection has departed from them, and the LORD is with us. Do not fear them."* - Numbers 14:6-9

> *"And the LORD said to Joshua, "This day I will begin to exalt you in the sight of all Israel, that they may know that, as I was with Moses, so I will be with you." - Joshua 3:7*

Elisha was another one who served Elijah such that his service was remembered even after the death of Elijah. Three kings were in desperate need of water for themselves and their cattle, only God's divine intervention would save them from calamity. Jehoshaphat requested if there is a prophet in town, people recommended Elisha and described him as someone who pours water in the hands of Elijah, one of the basic services Elisha performed was to pour water yet the word of the Lord was with him. He served Elijah well till Elijah was taken away from the world. No wonder he was rewarded with double portion of Elijah's anointing. You can't beat servanthood anytime.

> *"But Jehoshaphat said, "Is there no prophet of the LORD here that we may inquire of the LORD by him?" So one of the servants of the king of Israel answered and said, "Elisha the son of Shaphat is here, who poured water on the hands of Elijah." - 2 Kings 3:11*

The Lord said whoever wants to be a leader must first be a servant. There were other sons of prophets but they remembered Elisha pouring water in the hands of Elijah. To be promotion-ready, be of service at work, be available. Let people know you are around; let your boss know they can count on you and no job is too small for you. Sometimes the things we think are insignificant are the very thing that will tip things in our favour.

I remember one time when management was debating between retaining me or another guy, I was told we were on par, then one of the leaders said there was a particular item I could do and not the other guy. To date I can't remember exactly when I carried out that duty or what it was for that matter! God is able. What you think is your norm for being detailed may just be what the boss needs to make some decisions. Keep being yourself and let your work speak for itself.

## The Presence and Favour of God Triggers Promotion

Jabez prayed that the hand of the Lord would be upon him. That should be our daily prayer, *"let Your presence be with me let your favour rest upon me"*.

Joseph had the favour of God on him; people were able to see that God was with him, everything he laid his hands prospered by the power of the Lord (Genesis 39:1-6). God blessed him with ability and insight into how to govern. Joseph also honoured God with his lifestyle; he did not compromise. When temptation came, he fled, he said *I do not want to sin against my boss and my God* (Genesis 39:7-9). It got him into trouble but in the end he was remembered and was lifted up. So shall yours be in Jesus name. You will be remembered for good where people have lied against you or mistreated you or denied you that promotion, God will elevate you.

The favour of God also rested on Daniel and he was promoted (Daniel 2:46-49) but when it was time to go to another level, out of jealousy people ganged up on him because of his faith in God (Daniel 6:1-5); they threw him into a lions' den but God shut the lions' mouth and Daniel was delivered. In the end he was promoted (Daniel 6:17-28).

## Seek Promotion God's Way

Don't seek promotion by compromising your faith or doing something dubious. Proverbs 15:16 says *"Better is a little with the fear of the LORD, than great treasure with trouble. It is better to work hard and progress steadily than seeking promotion by giving bribes or falsifying certificates Proverbs 28:6 says "Better is the poor who walks in his integrity Than one perverse in his ways, though he be rich."*

There have been people who end up having affairs with their bosses to get a headway and when the affairs ends, the situation becomes messy and employment terminated. Proverbs 13:11 says *"Wealth gained by dishonesty will be diminished, But he who gathers by labour will increase."*

## Take the Challenge

Goliath came to taunt the children of Israel and King Saul but whilst everybody was scared, David, an errand boy, heard the taunts and became very indignant about Goliath's rhetoric against the armies of the living God.

There were many soldiers who heard the same thing day-in, day-out but it was a teenage boy who, by faith in God, was willing and able to tackle Goliath. God is looking for one person who will stand up in the strength of God and dare take up the challenge. Even the king wanted to put an armour on the David but David said he had not tried it before and he put on the armour he was used to in the strength of God. He was duly rewarded.

Are you shying away from challenging tasks at work due to the risk of failure? To set yourself apart, you need to step forward and take the bull by the horns.

At one of the projects I worked on, there was a challenging piece of work people tend to shy away from because if it goes wrong, there were huge consequences. I had attempted it before but not on a grand scale. When one of the key players was leaving, I was asked to take it over. I accepted but I knew it had to be God who would have to help me. It was later that I was told that was one of the reasons they extended my contract was because others were reluctant in handling that piece of work.

I had to stand on the word of God – Philippians 4:13 "*I can do all things through Christ Who strengthens me*". Many times we have to overcome our own fear and the effects of other people's behaviour. David had to overcome the ridicules from his brothers when he said he was going to fight Goliath. Others in the office too may make insinuating remarks if they find us attempting to do some challenging work, remember they didn't employ you; you are answerable to your boss and above all to God.

David's victory thrust him into the limelight, facing Goliath became his platform to greatness. What you are dreading maybe the set up for your promotion; so take courage and face the challenge. Victory is yours in Jesus' Name.

# CHAPTER 9

# PREPARING FOR RETIREMENT

I feel it will be inappropriate to end the book without talking about retirement. It is often said that **we don't, retire we re-fire** but I believe as we get to our golden years, we need to enter a season where we have a choice which type of work we get involved in and how many hours we want to work. To be able to have that choice we need to prepare for it just like the example given to us in the word of God about the ants.

> *"Go to the ant, you sluggard! Consider her ways and be wise, which, having no captain, Overseer or ruler, 8 provides her supplies in the summer, and gathers her food in the harvest." - Proverbs 6:6-8*

Ants have no captain to watch over them, yet they do what they are supposed to do; they are organised, planned and understood the season when to sow and when to harvest. They knew that at a particular time (winter) there will be no provision, so their vision or goal is to make provision for winter. For them to achieve their goal, they planned. The plan or strategy is to collect as much as they can in summer i.e. save up. Of course in doing this they have to analyse their resources, what are they going to need, manpower and building for storage.

By virtue of the goal they have in mind, and the plan they have already established, they are able to focus and achieve their desired goal despite obstacles they might find on their ways.

> *"... sons of Issachar who had understanding of the times, to know what Israel ought to do ..." – 1 Chronicles 12:32*

Have we studied when the summertime of our lives is, there are some things you can do at 30, 40 which you cannot do at 70. Usually you'll find people tend to be more active building their careers, work hard at their businesses etc. so that when they are 65 they are still not loaded with mortgage payments etc. They work hard and then rest later, I am not advocating older people cannot keep on working past 65, I am just saying at that time in your life, except if something had drastically gone wrong, you should be retiring and working for leisure rather than because you have to work. There is a difference when you are debt-free and you are working to keep active rather than you having to work to just pay for things you should have done away with.

Some of us think we can succeed in life by *playing it by ear.* No goals, no planning about the future, we just sleep and wake up, go to work and take whatever is given to us then we say life is not fair.

We need to have a vision for our golden years and plan towards it. When do you want to retire? At 50, 60, 70 years old? How old are you now? How many years do you have to go before you reach your projected retirement year?

> *"Where there is no revelation (vision) the people cast off restraints (my people perish)" - Proverbs 29:18*

Our God is a God Who plans. He is a God of order not an author of chaos and confusion. At creation, He knew what should be created first before human beings. We charismatic have tried to hide under the notion 'as the spirit leads' to avoid accountability. When the Spirit leads everything else bows and everybody will know.

God had a plan about the world and when it was completed He looked at it, gave an evaluation and rested.

> *"Then God saw everything that He had made and indeed it was very good. So the evening and the morning were the sixth day." Genesis 1:31*

> *"And on the seventh day God ended His work, which He had done, and He rested on the seventh day from all His work which He had done." Genesis 2:2*

Interestingly, God rested on the 7th day, I am inclined to say our 70s should be our season of rest and continue to pursue the things of God in training those who are coming behind.

We need to be forward acting today. We need to begin putting things in place today for tomorrow and not let tomorrow arrive as a surprise. Part of planning is to know how much you will need when you stop working. If your current household income is £3000 a month as a couple, when you retire in UK at a pensionable age, you might get state pension of £600 each if you have paid the maximum National Insurance Contributions. If you do not have other company pension, are you able to live on £1200 a month as a couple or £600 as a single person? Currently the UK will help out with pension credit if your income is low but the law is changing no one knows what tomorrow will bring.

So you need to plan such that by the time you reach pensionable age, your expenditure is less than projected income or else there maybe challenges ahead. During the time of plenty by the revelation and ingenuity of God, Joseph prepared Egypt for 7 years of famine during 7 years of plenty. Whilst you have the resources now, start putting something away for the golden years. Some people do this by:

a) Paying off their mortgages early by the time they are 50-55 either by paying extra every month on their mortgage payment or paying a lump sum every year. Also shopping around for bargains and ploughing back anything saved into the mortgage. I remember I shopped around for house insurance and managed to get it 40% cheaper, the saving of about £300 a year, which is a significant amount to add to a mortgage.
b) Buy a second property as an investment which they pay off before reaching retirement so that the rent becomes an income at retirement.
c) Pay into government tax free saving schemes like ISA.
d) Contribute towards your company pension scheme and if they do not have one, register with the government pension schemes or other reputable pension providers.
e) Savings – set up funds for different life expenditures. Emergency fund, holiday fund, retirement fund, children's help fund (nowadays parents tend to help their children for weddings, house deposit, grandchildren college fees etc.). You need to plan for it so that it doesn't come as a surprise. The older you get and the fewer the years you've got to achieve your goal, the more creative and aggressive you need to become in your preparation. The Internet is full of different ideas that help people save. Savings does not mean you don't enjoy life, it just mean shopping around to find bargains. One of my sisters is very good in finding holiday bargain including using her supermarket vouchers and air miles points where she can.
f) Multiple streams of income – Whilst working, people tend to develop different businesses to be operated part-time whilst not giving up their normal day to day job so that by the time they retire, they can still have an income coming in

Seek the advice of reputable financial planners for guidance ensuring they are registered with financial regulators as there are so many scammers who prey on people. Be careful of get rich quickly schemes and taking undue risk; those schemes where they promise to multiply your investments at an alarming rate – Proverbs 20:21 "*An inheritance gained hastily at the beginning will not be blessed at the end.*"

In all things pray and seek the face of the Lord that you will not be duped. Only God can give us wisdom to know how to navigate the future but doing nothing because of fear is not wise. You can check the following websites for some helpful information on money matters:
https://www.pensionsadvisoryservice.org.uk,
https://www.gov.uk/check-state-pension,
https://www.moneyadviceservice.org.uk for helpful information.

Of course there are issues in life that happens due to wrong choices or unfortunate circumstances beyond our control and we get to retirement age still in debt and nothing planned. This is where we need God's divine intervention, like the widow in 2 Kings 4. Proverbs 13:22 says "*a good man leaves an inheritance for his children's children*" however in this case, there was no inheritance but debt. This woman cried out to Elisha to say creditors are coming to take her children, she didn't accept the notion of "*Que sera, sera, whatever will be, will be*"; she cried out for help. We need to cry out to the Lord even when everything is messy and there seems to be no way out.

The Lord gave this woman a miracle by multiplying what she had in the house. As you present your condition to the Lord and the little you have, God is able to multiply it and meet you at the point of the need. She was told to go and sell the produce and pay off her debt and live on the rest. God is able to turn around our situations if we call on Him.

He said *call on me in the day of trouble and I will show you great and mighty things.*

You may feel your years have gone, your time wasted and resources squandered but God is a God of turnarounds. He will not allow you to be put to shame as you trust in Him.

## CHAPTER 10

# PRAYER POINTS AND PROMISES FROM THE WORD

These are some of scriptures that I have found so helpful in my career. Scriptures that I have prayed and promises that I have reminded God about. I love praying the scriptures, God said bring words back to me (Hosea 14:2).

God's words have the power to accomplish the reason why it was sent (Isaiah 55:11) and He watches over His word to perform it (Jeremiah 1:12).

> *"Take words with you, and return to the LORD. Say to Him, take away all iniquity; Receive us graciously, for we will offer the sacrifices of our lips" - Hosea 14: 2*

> *"So shall My word be that goes forth from My mouth; It shall not return to Me void, But it shall accomplish what I please, and it shall prosper in the thing for which I sent it." - 1saiah 55:11*

> *"Then said the LORD unto me, Thou hast well seen: for I will hasten my word to perform it." - Jeremiah 1:12*

As you confess His word over your situation, the word of God will prevail and you will experience victory in Jesus's Name.

## Favour

> *"May the favor of the Lord our God rest upon us; establish the work of our hands for us- yes, establish the work of our hands."*- Psalm 90:17

> *"For thou, Lord, wilt bless the righteous; with favour wilt thou compass him as with a shield." - Psalm 5:12*

> *"Remember me, O LORD, with the favour You have toward Your people. Oh, visit me with Your salvation." - Psalm 106:4*

> *"You will arise and have mercy on Zion; for the time to favour her, yes, the set time, has come."- Psalms 102:13*

> *"Let not mercy and truth forsake thee... so shall thou find favour and good understanding in the sight of God and man." - Proverbs 3: 3-4*

> *"He who earnestly seeks good finds favour..." - Proverbs 11:27a*

***Jesus*** *grew in favour with God and man (Luke 2:52).*
***Daniel*** *had favour and goodwill of the chief of the eunuch (Daniel 1:9).*
***Joseph*** *had favour with his master Potiphar (Genesis 39:4), with the prison warden (Genesis 39:21).*
***Samuel*** *grew in favour (1 Samuel 2:26).*
***Ruth*** *had favour with Boaz (Ruth 2:1-19).*
***Esther*** *had favour with the king (Esther 2:9, 15, 17).*
***Nehemiah*** *had favour with the king (Nehemiah 1:11, 2:5).*
***Israelites*** *had favour with the Egyptians (Exodus 12:36).*

**I thank You Father for blessing me with favour as I stand in the righteousness of our Lord Jesus Christ. Thank You**

Lord for surrounding me with favour as a shield in my going out and coming in; in my rising and lying down. I am favoured therefore I will not be disadvantaged. Let Your favour rest upon me mightily and establish the work of my hands at -------- , where things have been unstable in my department, please establish it, show me if there is anything I need to be doing to contribute to the work being establish.

Lord, help me to always be good to my employers and colleagues, help me not to retaliate when I have been offended; for goodness is one of the fruit of the spirit and I want to be obedient to you.

Father, I have been good to this company, I have diligently carried out my assignment to the best of my ability, dear Lord remember me and favour me. I stand on Your word oh God that You will favour me now as they determine who will be retained or be let go. Lord help me to always walk in mercy and truth so that favour and good understanding will be my portion.

Nehemiah, Esther, Joseph, Daniel all had favour before the king; Father I receive favour in the eyes of those that matter, my boss (*name here*), director, my team mates, my clients etc. Lord, I grow in favour in this company as Jesus and Samuel grew in favour with both God and man. The favour You bestowed upon me when I joined this company will not diminish, I will not do something that will tarnish my reputation or Your Name. I receive favour as jobs are being allocated in my team just like Ruth had favour before Boaz' lead officers, I receive appropriate tasks.

I receive favour as I present my request to my boss for ---------------- *(list the things you are seeking your boss to approve)*. Your favour upon my life will trigger preferential treatment like Ester was giving more portions than the rest, like

**Daniel was allowed his diet. In the manner that Israelites were favoured before the Egyptians, Lord I receive favour as I approach the HR department or ---------------those who have withheld my wages or denied me pay rise.**

## Success and Promotion

*"Then the king promoted Daniel and gave him many great gifts…." - Daniel 2:48*

*"For exaltation comes neither from the east, nor from the west nor from the south. But God is the Judge: He puts down one, and exalts another." - Psalms 75:6-7*

*"This Book of the Law shall not depart from your mouth, but you shall meditate in it day and night, that you may observe to do according to all that is written in it. For then you will make your way prosperous, and then you will have good success." - Joshua 1:8*

*"And the LORD will make you the head and not the tail; you shall be above only, and not be beneath, if you heed the commandments of the LORD your God, which I command you today, and are careful to observe them." - Deuteronomy 28:13*

*"Then the hand of the LORD came upon Elijah; and he girded up his loins and ran ahead of Ahab to the entrance of Jezreel" - 1 Kings 18:46,*

*"And whatever you do, do it heartily, as to the Lord and not to men, knowing that from the Lord you will receive the reward of the inheritance; for you serve the Lord Christ." - Colossians 3: 23*

*"That night the king could not sleep. So one was commanded to bring the book of the records of the chronicles; and they were read before the king. [2] And it was found written that Mordecai had told of Bigthana and Teresh, two of the king's eunuchs, the doorkeepers who had sought to lay hands on King Ahasuerus. [3] Then the king said, "What honour or dignity has been bestowed on Mordecai for this?" And the king's servants who attended him said, "Nothing has been done for him." ...[6] So Haman came in, and the king asked him, "What shall be done for the man whom the king delights to honour?"....... 'Thus shall it be done to the man whom the king delights to honour!" - Esther 6:1-9*

**Dear Lord, remember me and touch the heart of my supervisor not to overlook me during the time of promotion. I will not be stagnant in one position nor be denied promotion for You are with me. I will cooperate with You oh God and do all things to Your glory, help me not to be lazy but to be diligent and work hard as unto You knowing You see all things and You will reward me accordingly. Thank you for lifting me up. I receive divine acceleration to catch up and overtake where I have been lagging behind my peers. Bring me to the memory of people where I need to be rewarded for promotion, create a scenario that will elevate me O God and give me the boldness to step up.**

## Wisdom

*"If any of you lacks wisdom, let him ask of God, who gives to all liberally and without reproach, and it will be given to him." - James 1:5*

*"And in all matters of wisdom and understanding about which the king examined them, he found them ten times better than all the magicians and astrologers who were in all his realm." - Daniel 1:20,*

*"So David went out wherever Saul sent him, and behaved wisely. And Saul set him over the men of war, and he was accepted in the sight of all the people and also in the sight of Saul's servants." - 1 Samuel 18:5*
*"And David behaved wisely in all his ways, and the LORD was with him. [15] Therefore, when Saul saw that he behaved very wisely, he was afraid of him." - 1 Samuel 18:14-15*

**Father, thank You for granting me wisdom beyond measure so as to know how to approach the issues in my department.**

**Thank you for distinguishing me among my peers because I have the wisdom of God. During examination I will not be found wanting, my memory is blessed and I will know how to answer the questions appropriately**

**As Your representative in my company, I choose to live for You and conduct myself wisely. I will not bring Your Name to disrepute, I will remember that I am the salt and light to this world. Thank You for giving me the wisdom in relating to difficult bosses or team members. Help me to honour them and grant me wisdom to know how to relate with them. I receive divine strategy to know how to deal with my boss including knowing when to change jobs.**

## Excellent Spirit

"Then this Daniel distinguished himself above the governors and satraps, because an excellent spirit

> *was* in him; and the king gave thought to setting him over the whole realm." - Daniel 6:3

**I receive the same excellent spirit that was in Daniel, the ability to be diligent in whatever I set my hands to do and be distinguished, honouring You in all my ways and not compromise. Help me to remember always that I am unique and an individual specially designed by God. I do not need to fear what man can do to me knowing You will deliver me and still set me on top.**

## Fruitfulness

> *"Then God blessed them, and God said to them, "Be fruitful and multiply; fill the earth and subdue it; have dominion over the fish of the sea, over the birds of the air, and over every living thing that moves on the earth." - Genesis 1:28*

> *"And he moved from there and dug another well, and they did not quarrel over it. So he called its name Rehoboth, because he said, "For now the LORD has made room for us, and we shall be fruitful in the land." – Genesis 26:22*

**The anointing to be fruitful and multiply rest on me O God. I shall not be barren but bear fruit in my season. I receive expansion in every area of my life. The empowerment to make a difference is resting on me in Jesus' Name. I am blessed wherever I go and whatever I touch.**

**Lord, every blockage and road works that I have experienced in my life will not stop me in moving forward. I receive grace to persevere to try again, to apply for jobs again; to try the project again for I know victory is mine and I shall be fruitful in the land.**

## Blessings and Profit

*"Moreover the profit of the land is for all; even the king is served from the field." - Ecclesiastes 5:9*

*"In all labour there is profit, but idle chatter leads only to poverty." - Proverbs 14:23*

*"For the LORD your God will bless you just as He promised you; you shall lend to many nations, but you shall not borrow; you shall reign over many nations, but they shall not reign over you." - Deuteronomy 15:6*

*"Blessed shall be the fruit of your body, the produce of your ground and the increase of your herds, the increase of your cattle and the offspring of your flocks. "Blessed shall be your basket and your kneading bowl. "The LORD will command the blessing on you in your storehouses and in all to which you set your hand, and He will bless you in the land which the LORD your God is giving you. ....... And the LORD will grant you plenty of goods, in the fruit of your body, in the increase of your livestock, and in the produce of your ground, in the land of which the LORD swore to your fathers to give you. The LORD will open to you His good treasure, the heavens, to give the rain to your land in its season, and to bless all the work of your hand. You shall lend to many nations, but you shall not borrow." - Deuteronomy 28:3-12*

*"The LORD your God will make you abound in all the work of your hand, in the fruit of your body, in the increase of your livestock, and in the produce of your land for good. For the LORD will again rejoice over*

*you for good as He rejoiced over your fathers" - Deuteronomy 30:9*

*"And let us not grow weary while doing good, for in due season we shall reap if we do not lose heart." - Galatians 6:9*

Father, the profit of the land (the country where you live, the company where you work for) is mine also and I will share in the profit. The land shall yield its increase unto me, I will be a partaker of the blessing. Lord bless the management of the company that they will make good decisions to the betterment of the company. Lord I thank You that I am blessed in every area of my life including the office where I work and the proceeds that come from the work. The enemy will not tamper with my resources and I will not labour for loss. I will be willing and obedient and eat the good of the land.

Thank You Lord that every project or task I am given to do is blessed and I will enjoy the profit in Jesus' Name.

## Power and Ability/Intelligence

*"And you shall remember the LORD your God, for it is He who gives you power to get wealth that He may establish His covenant which He swore to your fathers, as it is this day." - Deuteronomy 8:18*

*".......I am the LORD your God, Who teaches you to profit, Who leads you by the way you should go" - Isaiah 48:17.*

*"I can do all things through Christ who strengthen me." – Philippians 4:13*

*"As for these four young men, God gave them knowledge and skill in all literature and wisdom; and Daniel had understanding in all visions and dreams." - Daniel 1:17*

*"See, the LORD has called by name Bezalel ..... and He has filled him with the Spirit of God, in wisdom and understanding, in knowledge and all manner of workmanship, to design artistic works, to work in gold and silver and bronze, in cutting jewels for setting, in carving wood, and to work in all manner of artistic workmanship. "And He has put in his heart the ability to teach, in him and Aholiab the son of Ahisamach, of the tribe of Dan. He has filled them with skill to do all manner of work of the engraver and the designer and the tapestry maker...." - Exodus 35:30-35*

*I will have sufficiency in all things for every good work" - 2 Corinthians 9:8-10*

**I receive every resource be it financial, human, emotional, intellect to do my job and do it well to the glory of God. I receive the skills and intelligence to carry out my tasks to an excellent standard that will distinguish me from others. I will become proficient in my field that I will be able to teach others. Open my mind up to new insight and ideas O God so I can apply them to my work and make progress.**

## Protection and Deliverance

*"And the satraps, administrators, governors, and the king's counsellors gathered together, and they saw these men on whose bodies the fire had no power; the hair of their head was not singed nor were their garments affected, and the smell of fire was not on*

*them. Nebuchadnezzar spoke, saying, "Blessed be the God of Shadrach, Meshach, and Abed-Nego, who sent His Angel and delivered His servants who trusted in Him, and they have frustrated the king's word, and yielded their bodies, that they should not serve nor worship any god except their own God!" - Daniel 3:27-28,*

*"My God sent His angel and shut the lions' mouths, so that they have not hurt me, because I was found innocent before Him; and also, O king, I have done no wrong before you." - Daniel 6:22*

*"No weapon formed against you shall prosper, and every tongue which rises against you in judgment You shall condemn." - Isaiah 54:17*

*Then they cried out to the LORD in their trouble, And He saved them out of their distresses Ps 107:19*

*"... and that we may be delivered from unreasonable and wicked men; for not all have faith." - 2 Thessalonians 3:2*

**Father, every plan of the enemy to hurt me, destabilise me, perplex me, confuse me so that I am not able to function in my job, I cancel and bring those plans to nought. Whatever they are planning against me will not have impact over my life. I cry out to You today and I know You will deliver me, thank you that I would not be put to shame. Victory is mine all the way. Help me to continue to trust You and totally be confident of Your victory knowing You are able. Help me to realise You are with me always and I have nothing to fear.**

**Father, help me to choose my friends carefully and be delivered from deceptive people who appear friendly but do not have my best interest at heart. Grant me the spirit of discernment as I relate to people. Help me not fall into the**

**traps of the enemy. Help me to watch what I say to people, where boundaries need to be drawn, please give me wisdom to do that in Jesus' Name.**

## Divine Guidance and Instruction

> *"I will instruct you and teach you in the way you should go; I will guide you with My eye" - Psalms 32:8*
>
> *Manoah said, "Now let Your words come to pass! What will be the boy's rule of life, and his work?" - Judges 13:12*
>
> *"My sheep hear My voice, and I know them, and they follow Me." - John 10:27*
>
> *"The steps of a good man are ordered by the LORD, and He delights in his way" - Psalms 37:23*
>
> *"Then Daniel went to his house, and made the decision known to Hananiah, Mishael, and Azariah, his companions, that they might seek mercies from the God of heaven concerning this secret, so that Daniel and his companions might not perish with the rest of the wise men of Babylon. Then the secret was revealed to Daniel in a night vision. So Daniel blessed the God of heaven." - Daniel 2:17-19*

**Dear Lord, please be my Teacher and my Guide at my place of work. You know all things and nothing is hidden from You. Help me to hear and understand Your instructions that I might know which step to take.**

**Father, I know the plans You have towards me are of good (Jeremiah 29:11); please help me to discover my skillset, my talents and passion that are inbuilt in me from the**

foundations of the world (Ephesians 2:10) so that I can accomplish those plans. Reveal the hidden treasures inside me and help me to pursue it for You are the One Who causes me to will and do Your good pleasure (Philippians 2:13). Show me the next step in my career O God, I will not be a wanderer but I will listen to you to show me the way.

## Divine Help and Assistance

> *"Fear not, for I am with you; be not dismayed, for I am your God. I will strengthen you, Yes, I will help you, I will uphold you with My righteous right hand" - Isaiah 41:10*

> *"I will lift up my eyes to the hills — from whence comes my help? My help comes from the LORD, Who made heaven and earth." - Psalms 121:1-2*

> *"... So his fame spread far and wide, for he was marvellously helped till he became strong." - 2 Chronicles 26:15*

Thank You Lord for the marvellous help and assistance available to me through the power of Your Holy Spirit so I can accomplish and excel in all that I do. Help me not to lean on my own understanding or depend on my ability, help me to trust You for strength.

## Open doors

> *"Behold, I will do a new thing, now it shall spring forth; shall you not know it? I will even make a road*

*in the wilderness and rivers in the desert." - Isaiah 43:19*

*"... See, I have set before you an open door, and no one can shut it ..." - Revelation 3:8*

*"...To open before him the double doors, So that the gates will not be shut: [2] 'I will go before you and make the crooked laces[a] straight; I will break in pieces the gates of bronze And cut the bars of iron." - Isaiah 45:1-2*

*"Then she left, and went and gleaned in the field after the reapers. And she happened to come to the part of the field belonging to Boaz, who was of the family of Elimelech" - Ruth 2:3*

*"A man's gift makes room for him, and brings him before great men." - Proverbs 18:16*

*"Then she came and told the man of God. And he said, "Go, sell the oil and pay your debt; and you and your sons live on the rest." - 2 Kings 4:7*

*"Then she said, "Sit still, my daughter, until you know how the matter will turn out; for the man will not rest until he has concluded the matter this day" - Ruth 3:18*

**Thank You Lord for making a way where there seems to be no way though it looks like jobs are difficult to find. Lord You know the right door and where next I should go, please open it. Help me to be sensitive to Your will and use whatever means You wish to manifest this blessing whether they are my former colleagues or I will be head hunted or it's through my applications. Close every door that the**

enemy have opened for me no matter how nice they look. Let me not be enticed and be forcing open a door You have closed. Father create an opening for my skillset, You know how You've wired me, open a door that will be compatible to my skillset.

Help me Lord to exercise patience where there seems to be a delay, help me to wait for the perfect time. Where someone is deliberately wasting time to make a decision concerning my appointment, Lord touch their heart and give them no rest till they confirm the appointment.

Lord, let my skill set be appreciated and valued to secure my next appointment, bring me to the presence of the people that matter, let my CV be read by people who will make decision.

## Restoration

> *"So I will restore to you the years that the swarming locust has eaten …" - Joel 2:25*
>
> *"So David recovered all that the Amalekites had carried away, And nothing of theirs was lacking, either small or great, sons or daughters, spoil or anything which they had taken from them; David recovered all" - 1 Samuel 30:18-19,*
>
> *"So the man of God said, "Where did it fall?" And he showed him the place. So he cut off a stick, and threw it in there; and he made the iron float. [7] Therefore he said, "Pick it up for yourself." So he reached out his hand and took it." - 2 Kings 6:1-7*

*"So the king appointed a certain officer for her, saying, 'Restore all that was hers, and all the proceeds of the field from the day that she left the land until now.'" - 2 Kings 8:6*

*"And I will give this people favour in the sight of the Egyptians; and it shall be, when you go, that you shall not go empty-handed." - Exodus 3:21*

*"Now David said, "Is there still anyone who is left of the house of Saul that I may show him kindness for Jonathan's sake?" .... Then King David sent and brought him out of the house of Machir the son of Ammiel, from Lo Debar. [6] Now when Mephibosheth the son of Jonathan, the son of Saul, had come to David, he fell on his face and prostrated himself. Then David said, "Mephibosheth?" And he answered, "Here is your servant!" [7] So David said to him, "Do not fear, for I will surely show you kindness for Jonathan your father's sake, and will restore to you all the land of Saul your grandfather; and you shall eat bread at my table continually." - 2 Samuel 9:1-7*

*"Then the chief butler spoke to Pharaoh, saying: "I remember my faults this day. When Pharaoh was angry with his servants, and put me in custody in the house of the captain of the guard, both me and the chief baker, we each had a dream in one night, he and I. Each of us dreamed according to the interpretation of his own dream. Now there was a young Hebrew man with us there, a servant of the captain of the guard. And we told him, and he interpreted our dreams for us; to each man he interpreted according to his own dream. And it came to pass, just as he interpreted for us, so it happened. He restored me to my office, and he hanged him." Then Pharaoh sent and called Joseph, and they*

*brought him quickly out of the dungeon; and he shaved, changed his clothing, and came to Pharaoh." - Genesis 41:9-14*

**Father, where I have suffered losses as result of my mistakes, forgive me and cleanse me from all unrighteousness. Where it has been as a result of others' mistakes, Lord I forgive them and release them in Jesus' Name.**

**Father, turn my losses to gain, restore me financially like You did the Israelites for all back wages, restore me to the position where I belong. Let the people that matter remember me as David remember Mephibosheth. Let the restoration be so tangible that it will wipe away every memory of losses. Restore entitlements to me including proceeds like You did the Shunammite woman.**

**Daddy, years that the enemy have ravaged me and my family, restore those years and help us to recover all. Father speak to us and let us know how to approach the matters, raise people that will speak on our behalf.**

## Confronting Challenging Tasks

*"'Who are you, O Great Mountain? Before Zerubbabel you shall become a plain! And he shall bring forth the capstone with shouts of "Grace, grace to it!"' Moreover the word of the LORD came to me, saying "The hands of Zerubbabel Have laid the foundation of this temple; His hands shall also finish it." - Zachariah 4:7*

*"Hear my cry, O God; Attend to my prayer. 2 From the end of the earth I will cry to You, when my heart*

*is overwhelmed; Lead me to the rock that is higher than I." - Psalms 61:2*

*"... The righteous shall be bold as a lion." - Proverbs 28:1b*

**Father, I receive boldness in all that I do. Fear will not be my portion, it will not overwhelm me nor paralyze me. I will approach my projects with confidence knowing You are with me. Thank You for Your enabling grace and giving me the faith to speak to the mountains at work. Help me to believe Your word and confess Your word not what I feel but to declare the promises of God. Help me when things are tough to run to you knowing You are always available. Thank You Lord that the mountains are crumbling before me and valleys are being exalted.**

## Struggling to Finish Tasks or Projects

*"I am the Alpha and the Omega, the Beginning and the End," says the Lord, "who is and who was and who is to come, the Almighty." - Revelation 1:8*

*"Shall I bring to the time of birth, and not cause delivery?" says the LORD. "Shall I who cause delivery shut up the womb?" says your God" - Isaiah 66:9*

*"Being confident of this very thing, that He who has begun a good work in you will complete it until the day of Jesus Christ." - Philippians 1:6*

*"Thus Solomon finished the house of the LORD and the king's house; and Solomon successfully accomplished all that came into his heart to make in the house of the LORD and in his own house." - 2 Chronicles 7:11*

Father, I receive the *finisher anointing*, I will no longer be starting project and not completing them. Everything that seems to abort that which I start, I cancel in Jesus's name. I will not miscarry but carry to full term all my endeavours in Jesus Name. Thank you for the strength to give birth to all that you have placed in my heart. The ability to start and finish well is my portion. Thank You Lord that the good work You have started in me will be completed and I will be careful to give You all the glory.

# ABOUT THE AUTHOR

**Toyin Jama** is a dynamic preacher with a strong ministry of encouragement to the Body of Christ. She has ministered at different conferences and Conventions in USA, UK, Nigeria and Kenya. She is a co-pastor with her husband - Dr Joshua Jama at Good News Assembly, Manchester and coordinates Women of Purpose and Influence Annual Conferences

Toyin's 30+ years working career has spanned over three disciplines – Engineering, Education and IT. She started off as an Electrical Engineer working for different Government departments for 8 years, during which she obtained her Master Degree in Engineering and gained Chartered Status in Electrical Engineer. Due to Family Commitments she moved into Education for 5 years teaching Mathematics in secondary schools. As a teacher, she was able to set up Saturday and Summer schools teaching Mathematics, English and Science.

In the last 2 decades, Toyin has been working as an IT Consultant for various companies in UK, USA, Netherlands and Belgium. She is a Chartered IT Professional of British Computer Society and the Director of ESAP Consultancy Ltd – an IT Training and Consultancy Company.

In her spare time Toyin mentors both young and old helping them discover and achieve their potentials which led to the birth of Fresh Start Mentoring Scheme. She has authored a number of books including "**Put Your Moses in Basket**", "**Jubilee Prayer Journal**", "**7 Keys to Accomplishing Your Purpose**" and "**Oasis in the Valley**".

She is married to Dr Joshua Jama and blessed with children and grandchildren.

# BOOKS BY THE AUTHOR

**Oasis In The Valley**

*Principles of how to thrive during affliction*

ISBN: 978-1-906825-03-4

In this book, Toyin shares the principles that help you to thrive during a season of affliction whilst waiting for breakthrough. The principles that will help you pass through the valley of tears and make it an oasis containing refreshing water from the Lord to rejuvenate you and those around you.

**7 Keys To Accomplishing Your Purpose**

*With God You Can Make It Happen*

ISBN: 978-1-906825-02-7

The principles in the book can also be applied to different goals and objectives in life, from wanting to be debt free, to building an orphanage to building a church. It is time to start seeing your purpose, dreams, plans and desires accomplished.

**Jubilee Prayer Journal**
ISBN: 978-1-906825-01-0

This is a devotional that takes you through 50 days of prayer. It contains Prayer points and scriptural references in seven sections – Individual Life, Families, Your Local Church, Your City, Business, Finance and Employment, Other Ministries and Thanksgiving.

**Put Your Moses In The Basket**
ISBN 978-1-906825-00-3

The book contains strategies for handling perplexing, difficult and seemingly impossible situations. It encourages you to ***let go and let God.***

www.ingramcontent.com/pod-product-compliance
Ingram Content Group UK Ltd.
Pitfield, Milton Keynes, MK11 3LW, UK
UKHW020134250726
13967UKWH00002B/650

9 781906 825041